W9-CHK-799

POCKET *A* DVENTURES

ST. MARTIN
& ST. BARTS

Lynne Sullivan

HUNTER

HUNTER PUBLISHING, INC,
30 Mayfield Ave, Edison, NJ 08818
800-255-0343; fax 732-417-1744
www.hunterpublishing.com

Ulysses Travel Publications
4176 Saint-Denis, Montréal, Québec
Canada H2W 2M5
514-843-9882, ext. 2232; fax 514-843-9448

Windsor Books
The Boundary, Wheatley Road, Garsington
Oxford, OX44 9EJ England
01865-361122; fax 01865-361133

ISBN 13: 978-1-58843-696-2

Index by Nancy Wolff

Maps by Toni Carbone, © Hunter Publishing, Inc.

1   2   3   4

Contents

About the Author

Lynne Sullivan is passionate about Caribbean islands. As the author of a dozen best-selling travel guides on locations throughout the eastern Caribbean, she spends much of her time hopping from one island to another scouting out a variety of activities, attractions, shops, accommodations and restaurants. Her goal is to steer independent vacationers on any size budget to the best each island has to offer.

WWW.CARIBBEANGUIDE2.COM

Readers may check for updates and new information for each island on the author's web site.

Questions?

If you have a question about the eastern Caribbean or one of the individual islands, send your inquiry through the website, and the author will answer as quickly as possible.

We like to receive email from readers and opinions, experiences and reviews that may be of interest to others will be posted on the author's web site.

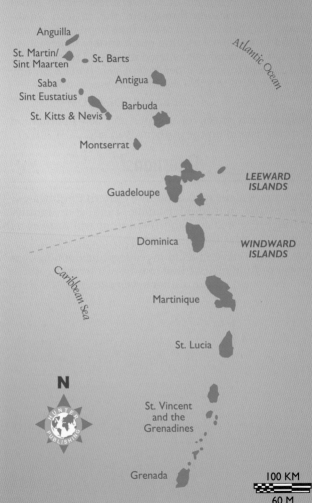

Lesser Antilles

Anguilla

St. Martin/
Sint Maarten · St. Barts

Saba ·
Sint Eustatius ·

St. Kitts & Nevis ·

Antigua

Barbuda

Montserrat ·

Atlantic Ocean

Guadeloupe

**LEEWARD
ISLANDS**

Dominica

**WINDWARD
ISLANDS**

Caribbean Sea

Martinique

St. Lucia

N

HUNTER
PUBLISHING

St. Vincent
and the
Grenadines

Grenada

100 KM

60 M

© 2007 HUNTER PUBLISHING, INC

Introduction

St. Barts and St. Martin are two of the most popular islands in the Caribbean. They are located 20 miles apart, 150 miles east (and slightly south) of Puerto Rico, at the top of an archipelago known as the Lesser Antilles.

Saint Barts is a tiny scrap of land covering about eight square miles. It's an overseas *région* of France, and old-timers still call it Saint-Barthélemy, but most everyone else refers to it as Saint Barts or Saint-Barth (the French abbreviation).

Saint Martin is several times larger, with about 36 square miles, divided almost equally between France (20 square miles) and the Netherlands (16 square miles). This is the smallest land area in the world to be governed by two nations. The Dutch call their part **Sint Maarten**. The French call theirs **Saint-Martin**. In this book, we use St. Martin to refer to the island as a whole.

St. Martin is easily reached from the US, and St. Barts is a quick inter-island hop by ferry or plane. You may want to divide your vacation between the two, or choose one island as your home base and take a day-trip to the other.

Which One's Best?

If you ask a dozen visitors who've stayed on both islands which they prefer, you'll get a half-dozen zealous votes for each. Those who favor St. Martin rave about the Dutch-side casinos, French-side restaurants, and sensational duty-free shops. St. Barts fans gush over luxurious little hotels, exquisite meals, chic boutiques, and camera-shy celebrities seen lounging on the beaches.

The Land & Sea

Geography, Topography & Ecology

Honestly, St. Barts and St. Martin are not gorgeous overall. Each has lovely areas, and both have stunning beaches and picturesque vistas, but don't expect breathtaking mountains, cascading waterfalls, lush rainforests, or idyllic rivers and lakes.

PRESERVING PARADISE

Eco-tourists probably will be happier elsewhere in the Caribbean, but St. Martin and St. Barts have made recent strides in the direction of protecting and enhancing what nature provided.

Most of the terrain on St. Martin is low, arid, and covered in desert vegetation or man-made structures. The southwestern part is dominated by **Simpson Bay Lagoon**, one of the largest landlocked bodies of water in the Caribbean; **Philipsburg**, the principal Dutch city, backs up to a huge salt pond. Rolling hills in the center of the island rise to 1,391 feet at **Pic Paradis** (called **Paradise Peak** by English speakers), and lovely bays with sandy beaches cut into the shoreline.

Tiny St. Barts has deep coves with long, golden-sand beaches that are protected from the elements by reefs and bluffs. They ring a dry, rocky interior topped by 938-foot **Morne du Vitet. Gustavia,** the capital, is built around a natural harbor prized by sailors seeking shelter for multi-million-dollar yachts. Smaller, well-groomed villages dress up the rolling countryside with charming houses, lovely gardens, and delightful shops. Lavish private vacation villas and year-round homes are tucked discretely among a scattering of palm trees and hibiscus bushes.

Weather

Temperatures

This is the Caribbean. The weather is perfect. You can count on a year-round average temperature of 77EF. Daytime highs occasionally reach 90E, but the average for January is 83E and July's standard is a balmy 86E. Nighttime temperatures have been recorded as low as 55°, but they are usually about 72° in January and 76° in July. The Caribbean Sea maintains a tem-

Introduction

perature of 80°, plus or minus a degree or two, throughout the year.

Rainfall

You'll notice a greater difference in seasonal rainfall. Summer, which runs from May through November, is rainy season. Winter, from December through April, is dry season. Both St. Martin and St. Barts have an arid terrain, but each still receives up to 40 inches of rain per year (about half of the amount that falls on greener islands). However, even during the wet season, most days have several hours of sunshine, and humidity is offset by steady trade winds.

 Residents of St. Martin and St. Barts say they enjoy a big season of small rains and a small season of big rains.

Hurricanes

Hurricanes and strong tropical storms get a lot of press, but the truth is that dangerous tempests are rare. Records show that most major hurricanes deteriorate at sea, and only one in three ever reaches land. In fact, you're more likely to encounter a severe storm on the eastern coast of the United States than in the Caribbean.

Plant Life

Wind and rain move across St. Martin and St. Barts from east to west, so the western side of both islands is drier than the eastern side. The arid hillsides have shallow, nutrient-poor soil that supports mostly cacti and succulents, but still, the countryside is lovely, especially after a rain shower when wild flowers burst into bloom and grasses turn deep green.

The eastern side of both islands is greener and sustains a variety of plants, trees, and bushes. A study conducted in 1994 classified hundreds of wild indigenous species, as well as naturalized flora that have adapted to local conditions. Although there are no tropical forests, several areas have woodlands with forest-like features. Sea-grape trees and palm trees grow in sandy soil along the shores, and a variety of mangroves and shrubs thrive in the salty water and mud found in coastal swamps and inland salt pans.

Some of the plants that are typically regarded as indigenous to the Caribbean were actually brought to the islands by Europeans. For example, the coconut palm was imported to the West Indies from the Pacific islands by British colonists who intended to harvest the fruit as a commercial crop. Today, a wide assortment of palm trees grow on all the Caribbean islands. They are characterized by compound leaves (called fronds) that top a trunk-like stem. New leaves grow from the middle of the stem, as older leaves bow outward and eventually fall off.

As you travel through St. Martin and St. Barts, look for these most abundant plants and trees growing in private gardens and on landscaped resort property, as well as in the countryside:

Flamboyant tree

Flamboyant trees, native to Madagascar, have small feathery leaves and clusters of red-orange flowers. The blooms last from May until September.

Frangipanis may be bushes or small trees. During the blooming season in summer, look for pointed waxy leaves and yellow, red, or white flowers with a scent similar to jasmine. The flowers are edible and sometimes used in desserts and jams, but the sap is toxic.

Latanier or **sabal palms** produce fronds used for weaving hats. Groves can be seen in Lorient on St. Barts.

Gaiac trees or **lignum vitae** are native to the Antilles. These small trees are now a protected species, but the wood was once used in construction. You will recognize this tree by its glossy green leaves, purple or blue flowers, and small decorative orange fruit.

Trumpet trees (also called poui or **poirier)** grow wild on the islands. They thrive in arid conditions. You will see their spectacular mauve, pink, or white flowers only from April to June.

Manchineel trees (also called **mancenillier** and **mancinella)** are tall, native to the West Indies, growing on beaches.

The sap from the manchineel tree is extremely caustic and can cause burns and blisters if it touches your skin or eyes. Don't stand under the tree during a rain shower, and don't pick up the apple-like fruit, which is extremely poisonous.

The anaconda or geranium tree is a Caribbean native with gorgeous red flowers that bloom in clustered bouquets year-round. Its fruit looks similar to white plums.

The **royal palm** is, as its name implies, a stately tree and the largest of the many varieties of palms. You will recognize it by its smooth, ringed trunk that bulges in the middle, and its thick fronds, which are made up of long, curved leaves.

Seagrape trees are the shrub-like plants that grow on beaches and along the shoreline. You can eat the small, reddish fruit that grows among the round, waxy leaves, but it's quite acidic.

Aloealoe vera is a succulent plant valued for its powerful medicinal qualities. Its sap is often used as a laxative and for soothing sunburned skin. Recognize it by its long, fleshy, serrated leaves that grow straight out of the ground.

Mamillaria nivosa is a round, fuzzy cactus with yellow thorns. It is endangered and rarely found on islands other than St. Barts, St. Martin, and Barbuda.

Yellow prickly pear is actually a cactus that produces an edible red fruit and bright yellow flowers.

Yucca

Yucca is native to Mexico and the southwestern United States. It has smooth, rigid stems that taper to a point; white flowers cluster in the middle of the plant from April to July.

Golden trumpet or **yellow bell** has a toxic, trumpet-shaped yellow flowers are toxic. You often see it climbing rock walls, and gardeners sometimes trim it into a shrub.

Purple allamanda is resistant to drought. Its large rose-colored flowers bloom year-round, making it popular with gardeners.

Bougainvillea is synonymous with the Caribbean. The robust thorny vine climbs and creeps everywhere and is easily recognized by its brilliantly colored bracts (leaves) that surround a tiny, inconspicuous white flower.

Hibiscus grows rampant in the Caribbean. The hardy shrub is often used as a hedge, and diverse varieties produce a profusion of colorful flowers. The spectacular blooms each last only one day.

Mexican creeper embraces fences, walls, signposts, and other plants. After a rain shower, the twining vine bursts forth with gorgeous pink flowers.

Oleander

Oleander flowers are toxic but lovely. The decorative shrub produces yellow, white, or pink blooms year-round.

Bengale clockvine, from India, and **bluebird vine**, from tropical areas of the Americas, produce hanging bouquets of flowers. You will see them growing wild along the roadsides.

ST. MARTIN'S LEGENDARY GUAVABERRIES

Guavaberry liqueur has been made in St. Martin homes for many generations, but in the mid-1990s it went commercial. The **Guavaberry Emporium,** located in an historic cedar house on Frontstreet in Philipsburg, is the primary retailer for the beloved folk drink, which is made from oak-aged rum and wild guavaberries.

Wildlife

St. Martin and St. Barts are not inhabited by indigenous land animals, but they do have a few imports. Europeans brought **mongooses** to the islands to eat

Mongoose

troublesome snakes and rats, but the skinny, long-tailed carnivores turned out to have a voracious appetite for beneficial reptiles and ground-nesting birds. Since there were no natural predators, the mongooses reproduced beyond expectations and became a real nuisance.

Iguanas were also brought to the islands by European colonists, but these large lizard-like creatures are rare and becoming rarer. You will probably see them only on resort grounds, where they are fed and treated as pets. While iguanas look prehistorically scary, with their spiny backs, they are strict vegetarians and don't care to share space with humans.

At sea, you may spot marine mammals such as **dolphins**, **porpoises**, and **whales**, which migrate through the area from December until May.

Turtles

Sea turtles, while not mammals, do breathe air, and you may see them swimming along the surface of the water. They live in the ocean, except when the females come onto land to lay eggs. All species are endangered and require 15 to 50 years to reach a reproductive age, so their nesting grounds on sandy beaches are protected by wildlife societies.

Leatherbacks, the largest of the sea turtles, have a leather-like skin over their backs instead of a shell.

Hawksbill turtles are recognized by their hawk-like beaks. They grow to about three feet in diameter and weigh an average of 130 pounds.

Green turtles have a rounded head and grow to about three feet in diameter. They live in tall sea grasses as they are herbivorous grazers.

Birds

Native and migrating birds are the islands' true wildlife treasure, and you don't need to be a birder to be impressed by the vast number and variety of species that live on or

Leatherback hatchling

migrate through the Lesser Antilles. They land on your table when you eat outdoors, tease you while you try to nap on the beach, and steal small items off your patio when you're not looking. The following will help you identify a few of the most common winged wildlife:

■ The **brown pelican** is grayish-brown with a long neck, long beak, and short legs. It's usually seen feeding along the shore.

■ **Magnificent frigate birds** (shown at right; magnificent is part of its name) have an extraordinary wingspan, which can reach more than six feet. They are jet-black, and you can discern their sex by the color of their throats. The males' are red; the females' are white.

■ The small **green-backed heron** has a distinctive call and gray-green feathers. The **great heron** has long legs and a long black feather growing from its white head.

■ **Snowy egrets** are white with black legs, while **cattle egrets** (usually sitting on cows) have white plumage and a tuft of orange feathers on their head.

■ The **kingfisher** is blue with a white breast and a ruffled tuft on its head. It dives into the surf to catch fish.

■ **Bananaquits** are little birds with dark feathers on its back and a bright yellow throat and breast.

■ Broad-winged **hawks** are frequently seen soaring in wooded areas.

■ Two species of **hummingbird** are often seen feeding among flowers: the **green-throated Carib** and the **Antillean-crested hummingbird**.

Bananaquit

■ Two types of dove live on the islands: **Zenaida doves** and **common turtledoves**.

■ **Royal and least terns** live on the islands. The royals are larger and have an orange bill. Their tails are forked.

 Fort Amsterdam, Pelican Key and Grand Etang on St. Martin are good places to observe terns and pelicans. St. Barts is home to 13 species of nesting Antilles birds.

Marine Life

The shallow warm waters surrounding St. Martin and St. Barts are teeming with life. **Conch** (say konk) is one of the most versatile and popular sea creatures. Their large, pearly-pink shells are favorite collector's items, and the meat is the key ingredient in many Caribbean recipes.

Among the vast number of fish that live in shallow waters close to shore, you're most likely to recognize the following species at popular scuba and snorkeling sites:

- **Sergeant majors**, a four- to six-inch fish with five black stripes around its body.
- **Blue chromis,** a brilliant blue three- to four-inch fish with big eyes and a thin deeply-forked tail.
- **Brown chromis** is a brownish-gray three- to six-inch fish with big eyes and a deeply-forked yellow-tipped tail and a yellow dorsal fin.
- **Surgeonfish** are six-12 inches long, blue-gray to dark brown, with lighter colors on their tails.

- **Blue tangs, above,** are blue with a white or yellow tail.
- **Trumpetfish** are thin and long, with a trumpet-like snout.

On shore, you're likely to spot:

- **Ghost crabs**. They never leave the beach, and during a full moon you can see hordes of them scampering about.

- **Hermit crabs** live on land, but lay their eggs in water. When they grow too big for their backpack homes, they look about for larger dwellings, and sometimes kill other hermits in order to steal their shells.

The People

Approximately 7,000 people live on eight square miles of land on St. Barts. Since the little island was settled by French citizens and never had economic motivation to open up to outsiders, 95% of its residents are white. The islanders are understandably friendly to tourists, but they have a reputation of being slow to accept newcomers. Illegal immigrants seeking work are quickly deported.

By comparison, St. Martin, with four times more land (36 square miles), has nearly 10 times as many residents (about 69,000). Approximately 70 nationalities are represented on the island, but most of the people trace their roots to Africa, France, or the Netherlands.

Language

The official language on St. Barts is **French**, spoken with a Norman accent, but most residents also speak English, either fluently or functionally. On St. Martin, the official languages are **Dutch** on the Dutch side and **French** on the French side, but most everyone on both sides speaks at least some English. You may hear a small segment of native islanders speaking a French-based patois among themselves. Some residents speak **Papiamento**, the unofficial, but preferred language on Aruba, Bonaire, and Curaçao – islands that are also members of The Kingdom of the Netherlands.

Cuisine

You will eat extremely well on St. Barts and on both sides of St. Martin. As you might expect, French and West Indian Creole are the most recognized cuisines on the two islands, but Dutch St. Martin has a variety of restaurants featuring Argentinian beef, Indonesian buffets, Mexican combination plates, and Italian pastas.

Everything, except local seafood, is imported. Meat, produce, and some fish are flown in from North America, while wine, cheese, and chocolate come from Europe. Small beach cafés and roadside stands specialize in grilled or fried fresh fish.

West Indian Créole dishes are a mouth-watering melding of French, African, and Indian recipes. You'll want to try the fried fritters, barbecued goat, spicy stuffed shrimp, and grilled langouste (the local lobster).

Common French & Creole Menu Items

Accras or Amarinades	Spicy doughnuts/fritters usually made from cod or other fish, but sometimes from vegetables.
Balaou	Small fried fish.
Bébélé	Dish made of boiled sheep tripe and green bananas.
Beignets	Donut-like sweet fritters.
Bière/bière pression	Beer/draft beer.
Blaff	Spicy lime-and-garlic bouillon used to cook fish. The word is said to come from the sound the fish makes as it hits the boiling liquid.
Blanc-manger	Coconut flan or gelatin dessert.
Boudin Noir	Blood sausage (made from pig's blood mixed with suet, bread crumbs and oatmeal) – not to be confused with Louisiana-style Boudin Blanc, made from pork, rice and onions.
Breadfruit	Large melon-like fruit.
Cabri	Small, bony goat, usually prepared as curry or smoked.
Calalou	Soup made with herbs, vegetables, crab, and pork.
Chadron	Sea urchin.
Chatrou	Small octopus.

Chou coco	Rare dish made from the heart of the coconut tree.
Christophine	Vegetable similar to a potato, particularly delicious when prepared au gratin.
Cirique	Small crab.
Colombo	Curry. In the Caribbean, usually a mild green curry, not as hot as Indian curry. The most common is made from cabri, small goat, but occasionally it's chicken or pork.
Corossol	A white-fleshed fruit.
Court-bouillon	Tomato, pepper, and onion mix.
Crabbe de terre	Land crab cooked with coconut and hot pepper.
Cribiches	Freshwater crayfish.
Déjeuner	Lunch.
Dombre	Small flour croquette.
Entrée	Appetizer, not main course.
Écrevisses	Freshwater crayfish.
Farci	Stuffed land crab.
Féroce	Avocado, hot pepper, and cod salad.
Fruit à pain	Breadfruit.
Giraumon	Pumpkin.
Igname	Any of a wide variety of yams.
Lambi	Conch, a large shellfish.
Langouste	Caribbean lobster, no claws.
Manioc	Cassava/tapioca flour.
Maracudja	Passion fruit.
Matoutou	Crab fricassée.
Migan	Mashed bananas and breadfruit.
Ouassous	Big freshwater crayfish.
Oursin	Sea urchin (chadron).

Pain	Bread.
Pâté en pot	Thick soup usually made with otherwise-unusable parts of a goat, vegetables, capers, white wine, and a splash of rum.
Patate douce	Sweet potato.
Petit déjeuner	Breakfast.
Schrub	A liqueur made by soaking oranges in rum.
Soudons	Sweet clams.
Souskai	Green fruits, grated and macerated in lime juice, salt and hot pepper.
Table d'hôte	Chef's specialty of the day.
Ti-nain	Small banana, cooked like a vegetable because it is not as sweet as the larger variety.
Ti-punch	Drink made of rum, sugar cane syrup, and lime.
Titiris	Tiny fish.
Touffé	Braised.
Z'habitants	Large crayfish.

Music

People in the Caribbean consider music their *true voice*. Most original rhythms are based on African beats and make extensive use of drums. The region has given birth to calypso, merengue, soca, zouk, and reggae, which have become popular world-wide. The common element in all these musical styles and their variations is an infectious dance rhythm and outrageous lyrics.

Often, favorite musicians and bands come out of competitions held during Carnival, an annual celebration on almost every Caribbean Island. On St. Martin, the annual Carnival competitions culminate in a play-off between 10 finalists and the defending Calypso Monarch from the past year.

On St. Barts and the French side of St. Martin, *Carnival* is celebrated before Lent; on the Dutch side of St. Martin, *Carnival* is celebrated after Easter. Residents of St. Barts put as much or more preparation into the celebration of their annual Music Festival each January and their annual Boubou's Festival each August. See page 18 for details on island festivals.

The 12-night **St. Barts Music Festival** (www. stbartsmusic festival.org) is held every year during mid- to late January. It features live performances by musicians and dancers in an informal setting. The audience is treated to ballet one evening, jazz the next, and perhaps a classical symphony the next. Performers come from internationally acclaimed orchestras, quartets, opera companies, and ballet troupes.

Boubou's Festival (www.boubous-festival.com) was started in 1999 by the well-known Parisian restaurateur, Christophe Barjetta (nicknamed Boubou), who owns several exotic eateries on St. Barts. The 12-night event in August is growing rapidly and features the music of lesser-known performers. As many as 1,000 spectators show up to enjoy the music each evening.

 For details on how to make calls on and to the islands, see page 28.

FOR INFORMATION & TICKETS TO EVENTS

Dutch St. Martin is represented by **Sint Maarten Tourism Office**, ☎ 800-786-2278 (in North America), 599-542-2337 (on-island), fax 599-542-2734, www.st-maarten. com.

French St. Martin is represented by **Office du Tourisme de Saint-Martin**, ☎ 0590-87-57-21 (on-island), fax 0590-87-56-43, www.st-martin.org.

St. Barts is represented by **Office Municipal du Tourisme de Saint-Barthèlemy**, ☎ 0590-27-87-27, fax 0590-27-74-47, www. saint-barths.com.

St. Martin and St. Barts - Significant Dates in History

Introduction

■ Pre-Columbian – Islands inhabited by Ciboney (Arawak-speaking) tribes from South America. People known as Caribs, were living on the islands when Columbus's ships arrived.

■ 1493 – St. Martin and St Barts first sighted by Europeans during Columbus's second voyage. St. Martin was named Isla de San Martin, after St. Martin of Tours, and St. Barts was called St. Bartolomé, after Columbus's brother.

■ 1631 – Dutch settle St. Martin and erect Fort Amsterdam. French colonize St. Barts.

■ 1638 – Spanish control St. Martin and build Old Spanish Fort at Point Blanche.

■ 1648 – French and Dutch gain control of St. Martin and amicably agree to divide it roughly in half and govern it separately.

■ 1651 – France sells St. Barts to the Knights of Malta.

■ 1656 – Carib natives revolt and take over St. Barts in a bloody coup.

■ 1659 – French resettle St. Barts.

■ 1650-1784 – Region overrun by pirates and privateers.

■ 1784 – St. Barts sold to Sweden.

■ 1794 – British troops take over French St. Martin.

■ 1816 – Treaty of Vienna grants St. Barts and French St. Martin to France.

■ 1848 – Slavery permanently ends on St. Barts and French St. Martin.

■ 1852 – Hurricane and fire cause residents to flee St. Barts.

■ 1863 – Slavery permanently ends on Dutch St. Maarten.

■ 1878 – St. Barts sold by Sweden to France.

■ 1943 – Princess Juliana International Airport opens on Dutch St. Maarten with the region's longest landing strip.

Travel Information

When to Go

Winter is the ideal time to visit. The weather is perfect. Lots of events are going on. Everything is open. But planes are packed, hotels are full, traffic is bad, and you must call well in advance to get a dinner reservation. All this, and prices are high too. Think about visiting during the shoulder seasons,

just after Easter until late June and again just after hurricane season but before the winter holidays. Summer is fine, too, but you'll have more rain – you may even encounter a tropical storm – and some businesses may be closed.

Airfares and hotel rates typically fall between April 15 and December 15, and many restaurants and shops drop their prices during that time as well.

Celebrations, Events & Holidays

Dates vary for some holidays and events, so all the tourist offices or check the official island websites to get the exact dates and ticket information for each event. **Sint Maarten Tourism Office**: ☎ 800-786-2278 (in North America), 599-542-2337 (on-island), fax 599-542-2734, www.st-maarten.com. **Office du Tourisme de Saint-Martin**: ☎ 0590-87-57-21 (on-island), fax 0590-87-56-43, www.st-martin.org. **Office Municipal du Tourisme de Saint-Barthèlemy**: ☎ 0590-27-87-27, fax 0590-27-74-47, www.saint-barths.com.

 B = St. Barts; D = Dutch St. Martin; F = French St. Martin.

January

January 1 **New Year's Day** (B/D/F)

Variable **St. Barts International Music Festival** (B): www.stbartsmusicfestival.org

February-March

Variable **Carnival** (B/F): Tourist Office

Variable **Ash Wednesday** (B/F)

Last day of Carnival.

April

Variable **Carnival** (D): Tourist Office

April 30 **Queen's Birthday** (D)

Variable **St. Barth Festival of Caribbean Cinema** (B): www.stbarthff.org

May

May 1 **Labor Day** (B/D/F)

May 8 **Remembrance Day/ Armistice Dat WWII** (B/F)

Variable **Ascencion Day** (B/D/F)

May 27 **Abolition of Slavery** (B/F)

Variable **Whitsun** (B/F)

July

July 14 **Bastille Day** (B/F)

July 21 **Victor Schoelcher Day** (B/F)

August

August 15 **Day of the Assumption** (B/F)

August 24 **Fête de Saint-Barthélemy** (B)

Variable **Boubou's Music Festival** (B): See page 15, *Music.*

November

November 1 **All Saints Day** (B/F)

November 11 **Remembrance Day/Armistice Day WWI** (B/F)

Saint Martin Day/Concordia Day (D/F)

December

December 25 **Christmas Day** (B/D/F)

December 26 **Boxing Day** (B/D/F)

December 31 **New Year's Eve** (B/D/F)

Carnival

On St. Barts and the French side of St. Martin, Carnival begins about two weeks before Shrove Tuesday, which is known as Fat Tuesday or *Mardi Gras.* Everything comes to a close on Ash Wednesday or *Mercredi des Cendres*, with the burning of *Vaval*, the King of Carnival.

The Dutch side of St. Martin postpones its Carnival until the last two weeks of April, so the island actually celebrates almost nonstop throughout the winter/spring season. The main parade is usually timed to coincide with Queen Juliana's birthday on April 30, a public holiday.

Travel Documents

When traveling outside the continental boundaries of your home country, always carry a valid passport. The **Western Hemisphere Travel Initiative** requires all travelers, including US citizens, to present a valid passport when entering or re-entering the United States Although you may not be asked to present it, immigration officials also require all visitors to St. Martin and St. Barts to possess a round-trip or onward-transit ticket, as well as proof of sufficient funds for their stay on the islands.

Get a Passport

Find out where to apply for a **US** passport by entering your zip code or state in the search box at www.iafdb. travel.state.gov, or use the automated phone service (35¢ per minute) at ☎ 877-487-2778. Additional information is available at www.travel.state.gov/passport_services.html.

Canadians can get passport information by contacting ☎ 800-567-6868, www.pptc.gc.ca.

UK citizens can call ☎ 0870-521-0410 or visit www. ukps.gov.uk.

Australians may apply for a passport at any post office in Australia or make inquiries at ☎ 131-232. Additional information is available at www.passports.gov. au.

If you lose your passport, contact the local police and the nearest embassy or consulate of your country in the Caribbean. Citizens of the United States can contact **US Consul General T.J. Rose** on Barbados, ☎ 246-431-0225, fax 246-431-0179, or call the **US Embassy** on Barbados, ☎ 246-436-4950. Canadian citizens should contact the **Consulate of Canada** on St. Martin, ☎ 599-544-5211, fax 599-544-3242. Travelers from the United Kingdom can contact the **British High Commission** on Barbados, ☎ 246-430-7836, fax 246-430-7860.

> *Remember that if you visit both islands, you will be required to present your documentation on each, even if you're just making a day-trip. However, there's no real border between the French and Dutch territories on St. Martin, so you don't have to show ID or declare purchases as you travel from one side to the other.*

Arrival

Foreign-made personal items taken out of the US are subject to duty each time they are brought back into the country. Avoid this expense by registering watches, cameras, and other expensive articles that shout "foreign" with the Customs Office before you leave the US. You can also carry the dated sales receipt, insurance policy, or jeweler's appraisal to prove prior possession. To find the nearest Customs Office, ☎ 202-354-1000, www.customs.gov.

Do not try to enter the Caribbean with illegal drugs, including marijuana. Possessing even a small amount will land you in jail and cost you more than you'll want to pay to get out. If you take prescription medications, carry them in the original labeled container, and if they contain narcotics, get a note from your doctor or carry a copy of the prescription.

Returning Home

Make your trip through Customs quick and hassle-free by packing all items that you bought on the islands together in the same bag and having all receipts readily available for Customs officials. Remember that you must declare everything that was given to you as a gift, as well as everything that you bought. If you had merchandise shipped home, you must declare these items when you go through Customs.

Citizens of the **UK** can obtain a copy of regulations by contacting the National Advice Service of The UK Customs and Excise Center, ☎ 0800-59-5000, www. hmce.gov.uk.

Canadians living in all provinces can get a summary of regulations by contacting the Canada Customs and Revenue Agency, ☎ 800-461-9999, www.ccra-adrc.gc. ca.

Each resident of the **United States** is allowed to return home with $600 worth of duty-free goods every 30 days. If you arrive with new items worth more than the allowable credit, you will be charged a flat rate of 10% on the excess.

US citizens who are at least 21 years old may reenter the country with one liter of duty-free alcohol, and all residents may bring back 200 cigarettes and 200 cigars, as long as the cigars are not from Cuba.

Up to $200 worth of duty-free merchandise may be sent home from abroad, but only one package may be sent to each address per day.

The government publishes a valuable pamphlet for travelers called ***Know Before You Go***. It's free, and may save you time, money, and stress when you travel outside the country. Request a copy from the US Customs Service, ☎ 202-354-1000, www.customs.gov.

 Tip: *Some airlines and inter-island boats include the tax in the ticket price. Ask when you purchase your tickets.*

Departure Tax

You will be charged a $30 departure tax when you leave St. Martin, even if you're going to St. Barts or one of the other nearby islands. The only exception is for travelers going to another island within the Netherlands Antilles, such as Saba or St. Eustatias, in which case the tax is only $10. Expect to pay your tax at a separate window after you check in, but before you enter the departure lounge.

St. Barts charges a $5 per person departure tax, when your next stop is another French island and $10 when you are going anywhere else. You must pay the tax in dollars or euros before departure.

Health & Safety

St. Martin and St. Barts are clean, modern, and safe. That said, there are some common precautions that you should take.

■ *The **water** that comes from indoor taps is desalinated sea water or purified rain water. It tastes fine. Restaurants will pretend that they do not serve tap water, but insist, unless you prefer bottled water, which may cost more than soda or wine. Do not drink water meant for irrigation from outdoor taps.*

■ *Food in almost all eating establishments is free of disease-causing bacteria and contamination. Avoid prepared food sold by street vendors, and wash all fresh fruits and vegetables before eating.*

> *If you become seriously ill or injured while on the islands, your country's consular or embassy office in the Caribbean may be able to assist you. Also, your health insurer and most major credit card companies can suggest names of qualified doctors and certified hospitals in the Caribbean. For a list of hospitals and medical clinics, see the Facts & Numbers section at the end of each island in this book.*

- *Check the following agencies for information about infection outbreaks, health concerns, and suggested vaccines:*

  The Bureau of Consular Affairs, www.state.gov/travelandbusiness.

  The US Centers for Disease Control and Prevention, ☎ 877-394-8747, fax 888-232-3299, www.cdc.gov/travel.

  The Medical Advisory Services for Travelers Abroad (MASTA) provides health tips and useful links for minimizing risks while traveling. www.masta.org.

  The World Health Organization, www.who.int.

  Health Canada, www.hc-sc.gc.ca.

- *Remember that the Caribbean* **sun** *is stronger than in North America or Europe. Wear a high sun-protection-factor (SPF), sunglasses, and a hat or visor during daylight hours. If you feel dizzy or develop a fever, headache, or nausea, you may have experienced sunstroke. Seek medical attention.*

- ***Mosquitoes*** *are usually kept away by the steady winds, but at night and on calm days, you may want to use an insect repellent containing DEET.*

Crime

Thieves are among us, even in paradise. Watch your valuables and always, always lock your car.

Money Matters

Currency

Businesses on both sides of St. Martin and throughout St. Barts accept US dollars, though they usually give change in local currency.

The best advice for everyone is to charge as much as possible to your credit card, and let the banks do the math. This will eliminate inaccurate exchange rates, you'll have a detailed record of where you spent your vacation money, and your pockets won't be loaded down with a variety of mixed currency.

If the merchant charges your purchase in euros or florins, check to be sure the use of local currency is clearly marked on the charge slip. It is to your advantage to be charged in local currency, because merchants use a less favorable conversion rate than banks when they write up the bill in US dollars.

 The prices given in this book are in US dollars. Before you leave home, check the current rate exchange on the Web at www. xe.com.

ATMs & Banks

ATMs are located throughout the islands, including outside the arrival terminal at Princess Juliana Airport on St. Martin, at the cruise-ship dock and Bobby's Marina in Philipsburg, and at banks in Philipsburg, Marigot, and Grand Case.

On St. Barts, ATMs are located at Banque Française Commerciale in Gustavia and St. Jean, and at Banque National de Paris in Gustavia, among other locations.

 Dutch-side ATMs dispense US dollars. French ATMs dispense euros. Some machines give you a choice of currency.

Banks on both sides of St. Martin and on St. Barts commonly close weekends and holidays. On St. Barts and French St. Martin, most banks are open Monday-Friday, 8 am-noon and 2-4 pm, but hours vary somewhat, especially in the afternoon. On Dutch St. Martin, banks operate Monday-Friday, 8:30 am-3:30 pm, and most stay open an hour later on Friday afternoon. The bank at Princess Juliana Airport is open daily, 8: 30 am-5:30 pm.

 If possible, avoid exchanging money at hotels or currency exchange offices. They don't charge a commission, but the exchange rate is worse than at banks or ATMs.

Going Metric

Pounds vs. Kilos	
1 kilogram	2.2046 pounds
1 pound	0.4536 kilograms
On the Road	
1 liter	1.06 quarts or 0.264 gallons
3.8 liters	4 quarts or one gallon
1.6 kilometers	1 mile
Is It Hot in Here?	
15°C	59°F
20°C	68°F
25°C	77°F
30°C	86°F
35°C	95°F

 It's easy to remember that 28°C = 82°F.

Electricity

On St. Barts and French St. Martin, electricity operates at 220 volts/60 cycles, as in Europe and South America. On Dutch St. Martin, electricity runs at 110 volts/60 cycles, as in the US and Canada. Many resorts provide a hair dryer and an electric shaver outlet in their bathrooms, but check before you leave home. Ask also about the plug, since you may need an adapter if the hotel has French or Dutch outlets.

Use a surge protector for sensitive equipment, such as computers, on both islands, and watch for overheating if you're using a convertor. Charge your dive and photographic equipment, such as strobes, at the regulated outlets at dive shops.

Time

St. Martin and St. Barts are both on Atlantic Standard Time, which is four hours earlier than Greenwich Mean Time. They do not observe Daylight Savings Time. When the US is in standard time, the islands are one hour later than Eastern Standard Time. When the US is observing Daylight Savings Time, it is the same time on the islands as in New York and other East Coast cities.

Telephones

Telephones, like currency, are an area where the French and Dutch don't jibe, thus making a simple thing quite difficult. The area code for **St. Barts** is **590**. The area code for **French St. Martin** is also **590**, but when you call the French side from the Dutch side you must dial 00, then 590, then 590 again, plus the six-digit number. (Example: 00-590-590-xx-xx-xx.)

When you call within the **French** overseas territory, you must dial a **0** before the area code. For example, if you are on the French side of St. Martin and wish to call St. Barts (or even next door), you must dial 0590 + six-digit number.

The area code for **Dutch** St. Martin is **599**, and when you call from the French side, you must dial 00 + 599 + the seven-digit number.

Got that?

Making an **international call** is simpler. From either Dutch or French St. Martin or St. Barts, access the international service by dialing 00, then enter the country code plus the number you wish to reach. To call the **US** or **Canada**, dial 00 + 1 + area code + the number. To call anywhere in **Great Britain**, dial 00 + 44 + the area code + the number. You can find all other country codes listed along with long-distance rates in the TELEDOM phone directory that's available at hotels.

You may have to wait for a second tone after dialing 00 before dialing the country code and local number, especially on St. Barts.

On-Island Phone Cards

Public phone booths don't accept coins. Use a **Télécarte**, which looks like a credit card, to make local and international calls when you're in **French** territory. Use a similar-looking **TELCard,** when you're on **Dutch** soil. This is less expensive than phoning from your hotel. You can buy a card on St. Barts at the post offices in Gustavia, St. Jean, and Lorient, and at the gas station near the airport. On St. Martin, TELCards are readily available at convenience stores, gas stations, and hotel desks on the Dutch side. A Télécarte may be harder to find on the French side, but most resorts and many shops in the larger towns have them.

 Major credit cards can be used for long distance calls from some phone booths on both islands, but the rates are higher than with a prepaid calling card.

To Call the Islands

To call from the US or Canada, dial 011 to get international service, then the area code (590 for St. Barts and French St. Martin; 599 for Dutch St. Martin) plus the on-island nine-digit number, which means dialing 590 twice. When calling the islands from Great Britain, dial 00 to get international service, then the area code plus the on-island nine-digit number, which means you will dial 590 twice. (Example 00-590-590-xx-xx-xx.)

 The number for directory assistance on Dutch St. Martin is 542-2211; on French St. Martin and St. Barts it is 1012.

Planning Your Trip

You can gather quite a stack of information online and by phone from the tourist information offices. Check with the on-island office for current events, new attractions, and special offers.

Tourism Offices

Information on the Web:
www.st-barths.com
www.st-martin.org
www.st-maarten.com.

In the US

Sint Maarten Tourist Office
675 Third Ave.
Suite 1807
New York, NY 10017
☎ 646-227-9440, fax 646-227-9448

In Canada

Sint Maarten Tourist Office

703 Evans Avenue
Suite 106
Toronto, Ontario
M9C 5E9

In England

Maison de la France

178 Piccadilly
London W1J 9AL
☎ 09068-244-123, fax 207-493-6594

On St. Martin

Sint Maarten Tourist Bureau

Imperial Building
23 Walter Nisbeth Road
Philipsburg
☎ 599-542-2337, fax 599-542-2734

Office du Tourisme de Saint-Martin

Route de Sandy Ground
Marigot
☎ 590-87-57-21, fax 590-87-56-43

On St. Barts

Office du Tourisme de Saint-Barthelemy

Quai du Général de Gaulle
Gustavia, 97095
☎ 590-27-87-27, fax 590-27-74-47

Making Reservations

Transportation and hotel rates change often and vary between vendors. You often can uncover bargains and packaged arrangements, especially off-season.

Once you make a decision, pay by credit card, which will give you some measure of protection and a means of protesting the charge if an airline, hotel, or travel agency goes out of business.

Insure Your Trip

Before you pay for any type of travel insurance, check your existing health and homeowner's policies to see if you're covered while on vacation. If you need additional coverage, consider one of the following health, trip, or lost-luggage insurers. Some travel agencies, tour organizers, and cruise lines offer their own insurance, which may allow you to cancel your trip for any reason without charge. However, remember that these types of policies will not help if the company itself goes bankrupt.

Traveler's Medical Assistance Insurance

 Never leave home without your ID card that shows proof of your health insurance coverage.

For a list of companies that sell travelers' health insurance, ask your travel agent or check the website maintained by the **US Department of State Bureau of Consular Affairs**: www.travel.state.gov. Click "International Travel" then scroll down the left side to

"Health Issues." Insurance companies are suggested at the bottom of the center section.

Getting There

By Air

Air service is frequent from several North American and European cities, and regional or commuter flights are available from San Juan and other islands within the Caribbean. St. Martin has two airports, **L'Espérance** (☎ 590-87-10-36) on the French side, and **Princess Juliana** (☎ 599-545-4211) on the Dutch side. Since L'Espérance (airport code SFG) only accepts small aircraft, most international visitors land at Princess Juliana (airport code SXM).

Tiny **St. Bart's Airport** (☎ 0590-27-65-41, airport code SBH), accepts small planes from St. Martin and Guadeloupe. It's also possible to take a ferry from St. Martin to St. Barts.

Airline Contact Information	
International Carriers	
Air Canada	☎ 888-247-2262 (US & Canada), 599-545-2372 (St. Martin), www.aircanada.ca
Air France	☎ 800-237-2747 (US/Canada), 599-545-4212 (St. Martin), www.airfrance.com
American Airlines/American Eagle	☎ 800-433-7300 (US/Canada), 599-545-2040 (SMX St. Martin), www.aa.com
Continental Airlines	☎ 800-525-0280 (US), www.continental.com, 599-545-3444 (St. Martin)
Delta Air Lines	☎ 800-221-1212 (US/Canada), 599-545-2545 (St. Martin), www.delta.com

KLM	☎ 800-374-7747 (US & Canada), 599-545-4747 (St. Martin), www.klm.com
Northwest Airlines	☎ 800-225-2525 (US), www.nwa.com
United Airlines	☎ 800-241-6522 (US), www.ual.com
US Airways	☎ 800-428-4322 (US), 599-545-4344 (St. Martin), www.usair.com
JetBlue	☎ 800-538-2583, www.jetblue.com

Regional & Commuter Airlines & Air Taxis

Air Culebra	☎ 787-460-7558 (San Juan), www.airculebra.com
Caribbean Star Airlines	☎ 800-744-7827 (in the Caribbean), 866-864-6272 (International), www.flycaribbeanstar.com
LIAT	☎ 800-780-5733 (US), 599-545-2403 (SMX St. Martin), www.liat.com
Winair	☎ 888-975-7888 (US & Canada), 590-27-61-01 (St. Barts), 599-545-2568 (St. Martin), www.newconcepts.ca

By Cruise Ship

Destinations change as new ships come on-line and cruise companies adjust their itineraries, but the following lines are most likely to offer stops on islands covered in this guide.

Cruise Lines

| American Canadian Caribbean Line | ☎ 800-556-7450 or 401-247-0955, www.accl-smallships.com |

Carnival Cruise Lines	☎ 888-CARNIVAL, www.carnival.com
Celebrity Cruises	☎ 800-722-5941, www.celebritycruises.com.
Cunard Line	☎ 800-728-6273, www.cunardline.com
Holland America	☎ 877-724-5425, www.hollandamerica.com
MSC Italian Cruises	☎ 888-278-4737, www.msccruisesusa.com
Norwegian Cruise Line	☎ 888-625-4292, www.ncl.com
Princess Cruises	☎ 800-774-6237, www.princess.com
Radisson Seven Setas	☎ 877-505-5370, www.rssc.com
Royal Caribbean Cruise Line	☎ 866-562-7625, www.royalcaribbean.com
Seabourn Cruise Line	☎ 800-929-9391, www.seabourn.com
Windjammer Barefoot Cruises	☎ 800-327-2601, www.winjammer.com

Package Vacations

Many visitors book a package deal that includes transportation and accommodations. Often, these bundled arrangements cost less than separately booked hotel or airfare.

Start with the airlines. They frequently throw in multi-night hotel arrangements at a great price when you book your flight. Or go the other way and check with the hotel of your choice for a package deal that includes airfare.

Getting Around

Hotels do not operate shuttle service to and from the airports, but taxis wait for arriving passengers just outside the arrival terminal, and most car rental companies will either deliver your car to you at the airport or pick you up and take you to their off-site location.

By Car

International Car Rental Companies	
Avis	☎ 800-331-1212, www.avis.com
Budget	☎ 800-472-3325, www.budget.com
Dollar	☎ 800-800-4000, www.dollar.com
Hertz	☎ 800-654-3131, www.hertz.com
National	☎ 800-328-4567, www.nationalcar.com
Thrifty	☎ 800-847-3489, www.thrifty.com

See Getting Around in each island's section for local numbers of international companies and listings for local rental agencies.

By Taxi

Taxis are plentiful at the airport and ferry docks on both islands. Drivers are licensed by either the Dutch or French government and carry a published rate sheet, which lists authorized fares between many common destinations, such as from the airport to major hotels. Ask to see it. Daytime rates apply from 7 am to 9 pm. An additional 25% is added to the base fare until midnight; 50% is added to the base fare from midnight to 7 am. If your destination isn't listed, negotiate a price before you get into the cab, confirm the currency and whether the rate is quoted per trip or per passenger.

Unless the driver overcharges, is rude, or takes you out of your way, add at least a 10% tip to the fare. Tip a little extra if the driver gives information about the island as you travel or helps you with your luggage (50¢ to $1 per bag is standard, depending on the size and weight of each piece). US dollars and local currency are accepted, but don't expect the driver to have change for large-denomination bills.

Most drivers will not allow you to get into their taxi wearing a wet swimsuit, so make sure you're dry and wearing some type of coverup.

The **Taxi Dispatch Hotline** number is 147 on St. Martin. You can also call individual taxi stands:

- in **Philipsburg**, Dutch St. Martin, ☎ 599-542-2359.
- at the **airport** on Dutch St. Martin, ☎ 599-5435-4317.
- in **Marigot**, French St. Martin, ☎ 0590-87-56-54.
- at the airport in **Grand Case**, French St. Martin, ☎ 0590-87-75-79; in **Gustavia**, St. Barts, ☎ 0590-27-66-31.
- in **St. Jean**, St. Barts, ☎ 0590-27-75-81.

By Mini-Van

Public transportation on St. Martin is by private mini-buses and vans, which travel the main roads between Philipsburg, Marigot, Grand Case, and the large residential areas. Fares are inexpensive – around $1 or $2, depending on the distance – but you may have to change vehicles several times to reach your destination. Since the service is used heavily by local workers, expect the buses/vans to be crowded during morning and afternoon transit times. Few or no vehicles provide service at night. There's no public transportation on St. Barts.

Inter-Island Ferries

Most people take a 10-minute, 15-mile airplane ride between St. Martin and St. Barts, but you also can take a ferry or high-speed catamaran for about $50-$60 round-trip, plus $7 port tax. If you love the sea, the trip is spectacular.

If you are prone to motion sickness don't go to St. Barts by sea. It is always rough, especially heading toward St. Barts when the winds are strong.

Rapid Explorer, a new $5 million catamaran, transports passengers between St. Martin and St. Bart in first-class luxury in about 40 minutes. The air-conditioned cabin features a snack bar and accommodates 150 passengers in comfortable airline-style seats.

Trips leave St. Martin daily from the Chesterfield Marina at Pointe Blanche. Return trips are from the harbor on St. Barts. Round-trip fare is €89 ($106) for adults and €45 ($58) for children up to 12 years of age. Schedules change seasonally, so contact one of the offices for the timetable and reservations, ☎ 590-27-60-33, fax 590-27-69-20 (St. Barts) or 599-542-9762, fax 599-542-9782 (St. Martin), www.rapidexplorer.com.

Voyager I and ***Voyager II*** are 125-passenger ferries that run a regular schedule between both Marigot and Philipsburg on St. Martin and Gustavia on St. Barts. They also offer scheduled trips to Saba. Make your reservation well in advance, especially during high season. Contact them at Bobby's Marina in Philipsburg, ☎ 599-542-4096, fax 599-542-2858, at the waterfront in Marigot, ☎ 059-87-10-68, fax 0590-29-34-79, or at the Port of Gustavia. ☎ 0590-27-54-10, fax 0590-29-34-79, www.voyager-st-barths.com.

The Edge is a 62-foot high-speed catamaran that leaves Pelican Marina on the Dutch side of St. Martin in the morning and returns from Gustavia in the afternoon. It makes the trip in 45-50 minutes, which is about half the time of the other ferries. A sister boat makes day-trips to Saba. Contact them for reservations through **Aqua Mania Adventures**, ☎ 599-544-2640, fax 599-544-2476, www.stmaarten-activities.com.

Marine Service offers charter boat service between St. Martin and St. Barts. Contact them at Gustavia Harbor, ☎ 0590-27-70-34, fax 0590-27-70-36, www.st-barths.com/marine.service/snorkleframe.html.

Gustavia Express travels between Gustavia on St. Barts and Anse Marcel on French St. Martin. ☎ 590-87-99-03.

ADVENTURE GUIDE TO THE STARS

Every site, attraction, shop, hotel and restaurant reviewed in this book has been evaluated by the author for its appeal factor. When the allure is better than good, you'll find a star ★ beside the name. If you find two stars ★★, the author was very impressed. Three stars ★★★ means WOW!

Stars may indicate "super value" or "amazing view" or "best burger ever." You just have to read the review to find out.

St. Martin

Planes from North America and Europe deliver hundreds of vacationers to St. Martin several times a day. Many more come by cruise ship. The tremendous attractions include great beaches, year-round sunshine and bargains at duty-free shops. Many North Americans come to St. Martin for a fast French fix without

the long plane ride or the hassle of communicating in a foreign language. Others set up headquarters on the easily reached island and make quick day-trips to the neighboring islands. Adventurous types simply love the fast-paced, highly developed, two-nation isle, and no other island in the Caribbean offers more choices.

Little St. Martin is divided in half and governed by two nations. There's no tangible border crossing between French Saint Martin to the north and Dutch Sint Maarten to the south, but you'll know when you cross from one to the other.

The Dutch specialize in high-rise glitz, big-time gambling, and rambunctious partying. The French have perfected the gentle art of bistro dining and boutique shopping.

Top Temptations

- **Duty-free shopping** in Philipsburg and Marigot.
- **Dining** on gourmet French food in Grand Case.
- **Sunbathing** at clothing-optional Orient Bay Beach.
- Escaping to a **luxurious villa**.

- **Diving and snorkeling** the marine reserves.
- **Hiking** Pic Paradis (Paradise Peak).
- **Picnicking** on Dutch cheese and French wine in an isolated cove.
- Studying ancient **Indian artifacts** in Marigot's Museum.
- Trying your luck at one of the **big casinos**.
- **Day-tripping** to St. Barts, Saba, Anguilla, and St. Eustatius.

Official Business

The Netherlands Antilles (St. Maarten, St. Eustatius, Saba, Aruba, Bonaire, and Curaçao) are part of the Kingdom of the Netherlands, which includes Holland, and Curaçao is the capital, granted political autonomy within the Kingdom of the Netherlands in 1954. Each island has its own Parliament and elects its own officials to manage domestic affairs, but depends on Holland for defense and foreign policies. A representative governor is appointed for a six-year term by the sovereign of the Netherlands.

In 1986, Aruba withdrew from the Netherlands Antilles and became an autonomous member of the Kingdom of the Netherlands.

> *Citizens of Dutch St. Martin are Dutch nationals and carry passports issued by the European Union. Citizens of French St. Martin are French nationals and carry passports issued by the European Union.*

French St. Martin is part of the *sous-préfecture* which includes Tintamarre and St. Barts and is overseen by the island of Guadeloupe.

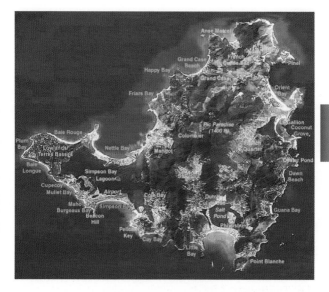

Getting There

By Air

See page 32 for airline contact information.

Unless you depart from another Caribbean island, you will arrive at **Princess Juliana International Airport** (SMX, ☎ 599-545-4211), located on the skinny strip of Dutch land that separates Simpson Bay from the Caribbean Sea. This is one of the busiest airports in the Caribbean (with the capacity to handle up to 2.5 million passengers per year) and one of the few in the region with landing strips long enough to accommodate jumbo jets.

The lower-level food court features Domino's Pizza and Quizno's, and the upstairs departure area has a full-service restaurant and 39 stores. Other passenger-friendly amenities include a bank, four ATMs and WiFi (wireless Internet) throughout the building.

St. Martin

St. Maarten/St. Martin
Map Key

1. La Samanna, Cupecoy Beach Club, Ocean Club, Sapphire Beach Club
2. Summit Resort Hotel
3. Towers at Mullet Bay
4. Royal Beach, Mercure Simson Beach, Nettlé Bay Beach Club, Anchorage Margot Hotel, Le Flamboyant Resort
5. Royal Islander, Maho Beach Hotel & Casino
6. Caravanserai Hotel
7. Horny Toad Guesthouse, La Chatelaine, Mary's Boon Beach Plantation
8. Flamingo Beach Resort, La Vista, Pelican Resort & Casino
9. Atrium Resort, Royal Palm Beach Club, Turquoise Shell
10. Carl's Unique Inn
11. Sea Breeze Hotel
12. Belair Beach Hotel, Divi Little Bay Beach Resort
13. Fort Amsterdam
14. Zoo Sint Maarten
15. Blue Beach, Captain Oliver's
16. Butterfly Farm
17. Club Orient
18. Cap Caraïbes, Esmeralda Resort, Green Cay Village, La Plantation
19. Alizéa
20. Anchorage Little Key, Hotel Mont Vernon
21. Le Méridien L'Habitation, Hotel Privilège, La Résidence de Lonvilliers
22. Privilège Resort & Spa
23. Grand Case Beach Club, L'Esplanade Caraïbes
24. Pavillon Beach
25. Mount Vernon Plantation

———— Paved Road   - - - - Border

············ Unpaved Road   Beaches

L'Espérance Airport (SFG, ☎ 590-87-10-36), on the French side, accepts smaller aircraft arriving from other islands within the Caribbean.

Getting Around

By Inter-Island Ferry

Rapid Explorer, ☎ 590-27-60-33 (St. Barts, 599-542-9762 (St. Martin).

Voyager I and **Voyager II**, ☎ 599-542-4096 (Philipsburg), 059-87-10-68 (Marigot), 0590-27-54-10 (Gustavia).

The Oyster Line, ☎ 0590-87-46-13.

The Edge, ☎ 599-544-2640.

Marine Service, ☎ 0590-27-70-34.

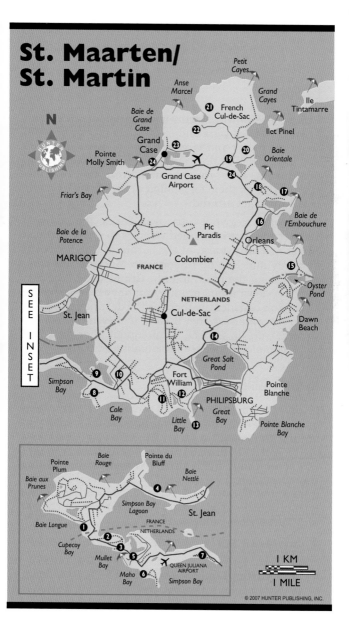

St. Maarten/
St. Martin

N

FRANCE

NETHERLANDS

Petit Cayes

Anse Marcel

Grand Cayes

Ile Tintamarre

Baie de Grand Case

French Cul-de-Sac ㉑

㉒

Ilet Pinel

Grand Case ㉓

Baie Orientale

Pointe Molly Smith

㉔

⑲ ⑳

Friar's Bay

Grand Case Airport

㉔

⑱

⑰

Baie de l'Embouchure

Baie de la Potence

Pic Paradis

⑯

MARIGOT

Colombier

Orleans

FRANCE

⑮

NETHERLANDS

Oyster Pond

St. Jean

Cul-de-Sac

Dawn Beach

SEE INSET

⑭

Great Salt Pond

⑨

⑩

Fort William

Pointe Blanche

Simpson Bay

⑧

⑪

⑫

PHILIPSBURG

Cole Bay

⑬

Great Bay

Pointe Blanche Bay

Little Bay

Baie Rouge

Pointe du Bluff

Pointe Plum

Baie Nettlé

Baie aux Prunes

④

Simpson Bay Lagoon

St. Jean

Baie Longue

①

FRANCE
NETHERLANDS

②

Cupecoy Bay

③

⑤

⑦

Mullet Bay

QUEEN JULIANA AIRPORT

Maho Bay

⑥

Simpson Bay

1 KM

1 MILE

© 2007 HUNTER PUBLISHING, INC.

You can find additional information about inter-island ferry service on page 36.

By Bus

Bus service on St. Martin is essentially nonexistent. Privately owned vans and mini-buses do run between the main towns and large residential areas, but they are meant for locals traveling to work, doctor's appointments, and grocery stores. You may certainly catch a ride on them for a dollar or two, but it's not the best way to get around.

If you want to give it a try, wait beside the bus-stop sign for the non-scheduled vehicles to arrive on Back Street in **Philipsburg**, at the corner of Rue Président Kennedy and Rue de Hollande in **Marigot**, and anywhere along the main road in **Grand Case**. You can also flag down a bus or mini-van anywhere along the road. (You can identify them by the destination sign in the front window.) They'll stop, if they have room to squeeze you in. Service is infrequent after dark and stops completely between midnight and 6 am.

By Limousine

If you're celebrating a special occasion, or just want a bit of pampering, hire a private chauffeur to motor you around the island in style. The following companies are on call 24 hours a day every day of the year to provide everything from airport transfers to wedding transportation or customized island tours. Rates vary from about $75 to $200 per hour ,depending on the type of vehicle used (luxury car, stretch limo or van) and the services requested.

■ *Caribbean VIP*, ☎ *599-545-5775, www.caribbean-vip.net.*

■ *St. Maarten Limousines*, ☎ *599-523-1814, www.stmaartenlimousines.com.*

- ***St. Martin Limo Service***, ☎ *590-690-88-52-60, www.stmartinlimo.com.*
- ***Prestigious Limousines***, ☎ *590-87-50-92 or 599-551-3990 (cell), www.prestigiouslimousine.com.*

By Taxi

The **Taxi Dispatch Hotline** number is 147. You can also call the individual taxi stands: in **Philipsburg**, Dutch St. Martin, ☎ 599-542-2359; at the **airport** on Dutch St. Martin, ☎ 599-5435-4317; in **Marigot**, French St. Martin, ☎ 0590-87-56-54; at the airport in **Grand Case**, French St. Martin, ☎ 0590-87-75-79.

Driving on St. Martin

Roads are in good condition on most parts of the island, and international road signs are posted, so getting around by car is easy. All the rental agencies will accept US, Canadian, or European licenses. You must have held the license for a minimum of two years.

Car Rental & Driving Tips

- Driving is on the **right** side of the road, as in the US and Canada.
- International **road signs** are posted along with local signs written in French, English, or Dutch.
- **Speed limits** are set in kilometers at 40 (25 mph) in urban areas, and 60 (37 mph) in rural areas.
- Most rental-car speedometers register in **kilometers**.
- **Right turns** are not allowed on red lights anywhere on the island.
- Plan to pay with a major credit card and ask before you leave home about included **insurance** on rentals charged to the card.
- If you pay cash, you will be required to leave a $500 **deposit**.
- **Age restrictions** for renters vary somewhat among companies, but in general, the minimum age is either 21 or 25 and the maximum is 65 to 70. If you

fall within these two age groups, verify the company policy before you book a car.

■ Always **lock your car doors** and use any theft-prevention device the rental company supplies. Don't leave valuables visible inside the car.

Rental Car Companies

Below are local contact numbers. See page 35 for international and toll-free telephone numbers and website addresses of major car rental companies.

Rental rates vary season-to-season, but they average about $35 per day for a small car with manual transmission, air conditioning and unlimited mileage. You pay about $65 per day for a larger car or one with automatic transmission or four-wheel-drive. Weekly rates are available and usually work out to be less per day. Insurance add-ons begin at $10 per day, but you may be responsible for $500 worth of damage anyway. Check before you sign up.

 If you decline insurance coverage offered by the agency, verify that the credit card you use covers you if you have an accident.

International Car Rental Companies	
Alamo	☎ 599-545-5546
Avis	☎ 599-2847 or 0590-87-50-60
Budget	☎ 599-545-4030, 0590-87-38-22
Dollar	☎ 599-545-3281
Europcar	☎ 599-544-2168, 0590-89-01-54
Hertz	☎ 599-545-4541, 0590-87-83-71
National	☎ 599-544-2168 (associated with Europcar)
Thrifty	☎ 599-545-2393

Local Car Rental Companies

Best Deal Car Rental	☎ 800-621-2865 (US), 599-545-3061
Cannegie Car Rental	☎ 599-545-3465
Executive Car Rental	☎ 599-545-4028
Route 66 Jeeps and SUVs	☎ 0590-29-65-88
Saint Louis Car Rental	☎ 0590-87-02-41
Sens Unique Smart Cars	☎ 0590-87-22-88
Valley Car Rental	☎ 599-557-2225, 0590-27-67-53

St. Martin

 Numbers beginning with area code 599 connect to an office on the Dutch side; numbers beginning with area code 0590 connect to an office on the French side.

By Scooter & Motorcycle

The best way to get around the island is by car, but St. Martin's roads are in good condition, so scooters and motorcycles are often used. Traffic in Philipsburg and Marigot is heavy, especially when a cruise ship is in port, and the main highways are busy during hours when locals are going to or from work. Unless you're a skilled, experienced biker, stick to side-roads.

You'll pay about $25 per day for a scooter, and $45 to $100 per day for a motorcycle. If you want to roar around the island on a Harley, plan to spend around $150 per day during high season.

Motorcycle Rentals

Eugène Moto	☎ 0590-29-65-89 or 0590-87-13-97
Location 2 Roues	☎ 0590-87-20-59
Super Bikes (Harley Davidson)	☎ 599-544-2704
Rodael Rental	☎ 599-542-5155

By Bicycle

While off-road riding is a popular sport on St. Martin, most streets have no shoulder and too much traffic to allow safe biking. If you want to bike to secluded beaches or tour the countryside, sign up for a guided tour with someone who knows the terrain. The following offer a variety of guided tours, kayak/bike combo trips, and bike rentals. You will pay about $18 per day to rent a mountain bike; $39-$49 for a two- or three-hour tour, including bike, helmet, and water bottle; and around $100 for a full-day combo trip that includes all equipment and lunch.

Bike Tours & Rentals	
Authentic French Tours	Marigot, ☎ 590-87-05-11, fax 590-87-99-47
Tri Sport	Airport Road, Simpson Bay, ☎ 599-545-4384, fax 599-545-4385, www.stmartinstmaarten.com/trisport

Getting Married

Honeymooning on St. Martin is terrific. Getting legally married there is another story. Don't consider a wedding on the French side, unless you're a French citizen. The requirements and paperwork are just too difficult. You can, however, have the official ceremony on the Dutch side and celebrate on the French side.

For 127 years, Dutch St. Martin had a law that prohibited non-residents from getting married on the island. But in 1997, this injunction was repealed, so you're free to tie the knot. Allow a couple of months to make plans and process the documents. A wedding consultant can save you time and headaches, and there are several on the island.

Tropical Weddings and Honeymoons, ask for Lucie Davis, ☎ 599-544-4143, fax 599-544-4143, www.sintmaarten-wedding.com.

Caribbean Wedding Consultants, ask for Joan Bethune or Marie Williams, ☎ 599-547-2067.

Enchanté Weddings, ask for Henneke Lee, ☎ 599-551-3449, fax 599-543-6007, www.enchanteweddings.com.

Weddings In St. Maarten, ask for Jean Rich, ☎ 599-557-5478, fax 599-544-3201, www.weddings-in-stmaarten.com.

Sint Maarten Marry-Me.com is obviously an online company, but they have an attentive live staff to handle every detail, ☎ 305-768-0233 (US), 599-542-2214, www.sintmaartenmarry-me.com.

DOCUMENTS YOU NEED TO GET HITCHED

You will be required to submit the following documents to the Chief Registrar at the Census Office on Soualiga Road in Philipsburg (☎ 599-542-2457, fax 599-542-4267):

■ A **birth certificate** for both the bride and groom bearing a raised official stamp.

■ A **declaration** of marital status for both the bride and groom that is no older than three months and stating that both are single. Forms are available from most attorneys, some notaries, and from wedding consultants.

■ People under 18 years of age, must have written **parental approval** for marriage.

■ The **legal address** of both the bride and groom.

■ Proof of **length of stay** on St. Martin (the bride and groom must be on the island for at least a week).

■ If either the bride or groom is widowed or divorced, he or she must provide **death** or **divorce certificates**.

■ Valid **passports** for both the bride and groom.

The official marriage will be performed by the Officer of the Civil Registry, but you can have a clergyman perform a religious service afterwards in the Marriage Hall of the Philipsburg Census Office. Marriages held outside of the Marriage Hall in Philipsburg must be

St. Martin

observed by six witnesses. Weddings inside the Marriage Hall require two witnesses.

Philipsburg panorama

Exploring the Island

Taxi Tours

If you want a private orientation tour of both sides of St. Martin, consider hiring a member of either the Dutch or French taxi association as a guide. You can find drivers at Wathey Square in Philipsburg or at the taxi kiosk near the waterfront market in Marigot. Staff members at your hotel reception desk and the owners or managers of good restaurants are another good source of guide recommendations. Be sure to request an English-speaking driver who knows both sides of the island well, and agree on a fee before you start out. Expect to pay about $35 for a two- to three-hour tour for two people. On a recent visit, drivers on the Dutch side were charging a bit less, so make a couple of calls and compare the itineraries before you decide on a

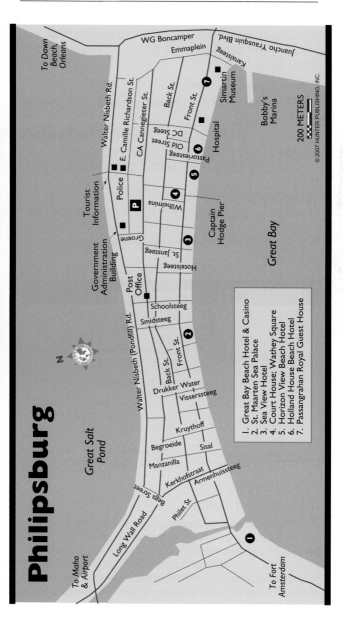

Philipsburg

1. Great Bay Beach Hotel & Casino
2. St. Maarten Sea Palace
3. Sea View Hotel
4. Court House; Wathey Square
5. Horizon View Beach Hotel
6. Holland House Beach Hotel
7. Passangrahan Royal Guest House

© 2007 HUNTER PUBLISHING, INC.

200 METERS

guide. You may also want to speak directly with the driver, either in person or by phone, to make sure you understand his accent.

Prince Personal Tours, ☎ 599-547-4264.

Dutch St. Maarten Taxi Association, ☎ 147 (hotline) or 599- 545-4317.

French St. Martin's Taxi Service & Information Center (Marigot), ☎ 590-87-78-87.

Top Quality Limousine, ☎ 599-557-5804.

Group Sightseeing Tours

Several reputable companies run scheduled sightseeing tours from both sides of the island. Be sure the tour you sign up for has an English-speaking or bilingual guide.

Tour Companies	
Transco	Quartier d'Orléans, ☎ 590-87-30-16, fax 590-87-39-30
Winston Sightseeing Tours	Quartier d'Orléans, ☎ 590-87-25-61, fax 590-87-25-6
Calypso Tours	Cole Bay, ☎ 599-544-2858, fax 599-544-2858
TriSport	Simpson Bay, ☎ 599-545-4384, fax 599-545-4385, www.trisportskm.com
Caribbean Duck Tours	Philipsburg, Front Street, ☎ 599-552-4637, www.caribbeanducktours.com

Independent Touring

If you have a car or motorcycle, you can easily tour the entire island in a day. This is good for cruise-ship passengers with limited time, but if you're staying for several days, consider dividing your tour into smaller excursions. Ideally, you'll want to schedule time to explore Philipsburg and Marigot at leisure, linger awhile in Grand Case, and take frequent beach breaks.

St. Martin

★ A Walking Tour of Philipsburg

The principal city of Dutch Sint Maarten is second only to Charlotte Amalie on St. Thomas (US Virgin Islands) for popularity among duty-free shoppers. If you don't stop to shop, you can walk the town and see its few sights in less than an hour. But no one ever walks through without stopping, so plan on spending most of a morning or afternoon browsing.

Philipsburg is built on a narrow stretch of land that separates the natural harbor of Great Bay from the marshy Great Salt Pond. John Philips, a Scotsman who served as a commander in the Dutch military, founded the town in 1763, and over the next 200 years residents survived by fishing and selling salt extracted from the pond. Back then, Philipsburg was wide enough for only two parallel streets, **Voorstraa**t, which bordered the sea, and **Achterstraat**, one block north bordering the Great Salt Pond. The principal public buildings were built around **De Ruyterplein**, the town square.

Today, landfill has almost doubled Philipsburg's width, and four roads now run parallel from one end of town to the other, but Voorstraat (now called **Front Street**) and Achterstraat (now called **Back Street**) still hold the most interest for visitors. Traffic travels one way, west to east, along Front and one way toward the west along Back. **Walter Nisbet Road** (also called **Pondfill Road**) brings traffic in and out of town along the southern edge of Great Salt Pond. **Cannegeiter Street**, also two-way, runs the length of town between Nisbet and Back. Narrow north-south lanes (*steegjes*) with names ending in *steeg* connect the four main thoroughfares.

PARKING

Parking is prohibited on Philipsburg's streets, but few signs tell you this. Avoid being towed by parking free near the police station on Walter Nesbeth Road. (Watch for signs pointing the way as you enter town.) Paid parking is available a block closer to Front Street at the corner of Peterson Street and Cannegieter Street, just south of the Government Building. Rates are $1 per hour, up to $14 for a full day. You also can park at the new public lot at Bobby's Marina on the waterfront at the east end of town. There is no charge for the first 20 minutes, then rates are $1 per hour. Some of the nearby shops and restaurants will validate your parking stub to allow free parking, if you buy something.

Wathey Square

A good place to begin your tour is **Cyrus Wathey** (say watty) **Square**, the former De Ruyterplein, site of **Captain Hodge Pier**, where shuttle boats drop off passengers from cruise ships docked in the harbor. The pier was given a $1.7 million makeover after Hurricane Luis ripped through the island in 1995, and tourist-friendly conveniences now include a tourist information office, an ATM, restrooms, and telephones. If a cruise ship is in port, the area will be especially crowded with taxi drivers, tour operators, hair-braiding artisans, and people hawking timeshares and fruit drinks.

Courthouse, Wathey Square

St. Martin

The covered pier sits opposite the historic and picturesque Courthouse, designed by John Handleigh and built first in 1792 by Willem Hendrik Rink, Dutch commander of the island, then rebuilt in 1825 after the original structure was damaged by a hurricane in 1819. The green-trimmed, white, two-story building faces the square. It is topped by a bell tower, surrounded by a quaint picket fence, and shaded by a palm tree. Over the years, it has been used as a fire station, prison, and a post office.

On the square, a signpost points the way to casinos, shops, and restaurants. Turn toward the east and follow the one-way automobile traffic along Front Street toward what is locally known as the "Head of Town." All the buildings face inward, toward the street, so you won't have the pleasure of walking along the lovely beach unless you turn down one of the narrow access passages or cut through a hotel lobby.

★Old Street is a personal favorite. This pedestrian-only shopping arcade is off the north side of Front Street, east of Wathey Square, between Colombian Emeralds and Oro de Sol jewelry stores. Plants and potted palms line the block-long lane that houses specialty boutiques and a French café.

Among the mostly characterless architecture of the duty-free shops, take notice of the few traditional buildings and gingerbread-design houses. The

Old Street

Pasanggrahan Hotel at 15 Front Street is the oldest inn on the island and the original structure was the home of St. Martin's first governor. Pasanggrahan is an Indonesian word meaning "guest house," and the West Indies-style inn hosted Queen Wilhelmina of the Netherlands for a short time during World War II when she was en route to Canada after being exiled from her country by the Nazis. Walk through the antiques-furnished lobby to the veranda facing Great Bay Beach, where you can enjoy a quiet drink, stop by Wilhelmina's old room (which has been converted into the Sydney Greenstreet Bar) or have lunch in the jungle-like setting of the hotel's restaurant (☎ 542-3588).

The **Guavaberry Emporium**, which occupies a late 18th-century cedar townhouse at 8-10 Front Street,

Guavaberry Emporium

was built on the site of a former synagogue. It's a busy place, with shoppers zipping in and out of the colorful old former governor's home to buy flavored liqueurs made with the local guavaberry fruit and rum. Old timers remember when the legendary folk liqueur was made in private homes and quaffed on holidays and during cultural celebrations. Stop in for a free sample of the bitter-sweet drink. If you like it, order a guavaberry colada to sip while you browse through the shop's other island-made products (☎ 542-2965, www.guavaberry.com).

The Sint Maarten Museum at Museum Arcade, 7 Front Street, occupies a restored two-story house built in the 1800s. Spend a few minutes looking over old photographs, antique maps, shards of Arawak pottery, plantation-era artifacts, items retrieved from the *HMS Proselyte* (a ship that sank off Fort Amsterdam in 1801), and an exhibit on damage caused by Hurricane Luis in 1995. You can browse the street-level gift shop without charge and visit the second-floor displays by paying a $1 fee (free for children). They are open Monday-Friday, 10 am-4 pm, and Saturday, 10 am-2 pm, ☎ 542-4917.

Just east of the museum, turn right toward the water into the ★**Sea Street Arcade**, a pedestrian-only brick-paved lane lined with specialty shops and cafés. Pick up a snack and carry it down to the sand, where you can watch men shelling conch. If your timing's right, you may spot one of the sailboats that competed in past America's Cup competitions leaving the docks at **Bobby's Marina** (☎ 542-2366) for a short-course race. You can sign up to join one of the crews for a three-hour sail by stopping at the **12 Metre Challenge** office (☎ 542-0045) at the marina. See *Adventures on Water*, page 85, for more information.

To get back to Cyrus Wathey Square, walk along ★**Great Bay Beach**, one of the nicest city beaches in the Caribbean. The beach is about 65 feet wide, and the mix of crushed shells and golden sand makes for easy strolling. On a clear day, you may be able to spot Saba in the distance.

★A Walking Tour of Marigot

The capital of French Saint Martin is far more charming than its Dutch counterpart, Philipsburg. But of course. *C'est Français, n'est-ce pas?*

Marigot (say *mar-ee-go*) means "backwater" in French and refers to the swampy conditions the first colonists found when they arrived on the island's western shore

St. Martin

View of Philipsburg

in the 1600s. If it weren't for the natural harbor provided by wind-protected Marigot Bay, the French
probably would have left the marshy mangrove to the
birds and settled elsewhere. But sailors then, as now,
were willing to suffer most anything for love of their
boats and the sea, so today we have a lovely town built
along the sandy curve of a yacht-filled bay.

Commercialism is less apparent here than in
Philipsburg, and for the most part, the town has re-
tained much of its innate French charm and West Indian style. Contemporary boutiques have moved into
colonial buildings and Creole homes, and new development blends esthetically with the old. A modern
shopping complex, anchored by a Match supermarket, is at the northeast edge of town, and the air-conditioned West Indies Shopping Mall and office
complex rises above the waterfront below Fort Saint-
Louis.

You can walk nonstop through the small town in
about an hour, but Marigot is meant to be savored
slowly in small sips. Allot an entire morning or afternoon for strolling through the shops and lingering

Marigot

over lunch. Return in the evening to dine by candle-light at one of the waterfront restaurants and enjoy nighttime entertainment.

 If you drive into town, park free in front of the Office du Tourisme on Rue du Morne, the road leading into town from Sandy Ground to the south, or in the waterfront lot near the market on Blvd. de France.

Begin your walking tour at the **Office du Tourisme** at the south end of town on the main road leading into town from Sandy Ground. Here you can pick up maps and brochures and ask one of the friendly English-speaking representatives for information. The office is open Monday-Friday, 8:30 am-1 pm and 2:30-5:30 pm; Saturday, 8 am-noon. ☎ 590-87-57-21.

Before you leave the area, stop by the history and archeology **museum** called **Sur les Traces des Arawaks** (On the Trail of the Arawaks), which shares a parking lot with the tourist office. Inside, the exhibits (labeled in English and French) include tools made from shells, pieces of pottery, and jewelry crafted by indigenous inhabitants as far back as 1800 BC. The pieces were dug up during archeological excavations made by the Hope Estate Archaeological Society and, by comparing their design, experts are able to link tribes that once lived on the island with natives of South America and follow their trail of migration from the Orinoco River basin in present-day Venezuela.

Other pre-Colombian exhibits include a reproduction of a 1,500-year-old burial site that was discovered at the excavation site in 1994. More recent history is depicted through numerous artifacts from the island's colonial period, and through photographs and antique maps from the last century. Contemporary local art and handmade crafts are displayed in the gift shop on the second floor. Ask about a group or private tour with one of the English-speaking guides, or visit on your own, 9 am-1 pm and 3-6 pm, Monday-Saturday, ☎ 590-29-22-84. Entrance fees are $5 for adults and $2 for children.

If you're interested in obtaining more information about the ongoing excavations at Hope Estate in the hills near Grand Case, contact the Archeological Society, ☎ 29-22-84.

★**Port Royale** is an easy walk from the Office du Tourisme and the museum. Just head north in the direction of town and watch for a passageway on your right that leads to the waterfront on Simpson Bay Lagoon. This is the best people-watching spot on the island. Lovely boats fill the marina, and boutiques and restaurants face the water along a U-shaped portion of the lagoon. You will feel as if you're in a small village on the French Riviera as you browse the chic shops, linger over café au lait at an outdoor café, or enjoy a gourmet meal at one of the petit restaurants. On Wednesday and Thursday evenings during high season, bands, jugglers, mimes, magicians, and dancers entertain along the boardwalk, and shops stay open late.

Leaving Port Royale, walk west toward the sea and turn north onto Boulevard de France, which parallels Marigot Bay. This will take you to a large square where

Marigot from Fort Saint-Louis

the **public market** is held on Wednesday and Saturday mornings. A taxi stand and public restrooms are nearby, and the busy harbor is across the street. Stop to admire the oversized statue of an island woman sitting at the head of the marketplace. This lovely piece was sculpted by Martin Lynn, who lives with his wife, Caribbean painter Gloria Lynn, on the main street in Grand Case.

Boulevard de France ends at Rue de la République, one of Marigot's best shopping streets. The new enclosed and air-conditioned **West Indies Mall** sits opposite the harbor, and the road stretches east past a serious assortment of sassy shops. Even if you don't want to buy anything, stroll up and down the narrow roads that run more or less parallel to each other south of République. (Rue de la Liberté, Rue Maurasse, and Rue du Général de Gaulle are the main streets.) The quality and quantity of French goods will impress you. If you get tired or bored, pop into a little bar for a glass of French wine.

Allow your energy level to dictate your route after you finish exploring downtown. If you're still going strong, follow Rue Fichaut north off Rue de la République to Rue de l'Eglise, which leads up the hill to ★**Fort Saint-Louis**, overlooking the harbor above the West Indies Mall. If you don't want to make the 10-minute uphill hike, return to your car and drive up. The view is terrific.

The French built the stone fort between 1767 and 1789, during the turbulent time that led up to the

Grand Case Beach Resort (Paul Sullivan)

French Revolution. British troops took advantage of the unstable political situation and slavery problems on St. Martin to attack and conquer the fort in 1794. The English held the fort, and controlled the island, for two years until Victor Hugues, backed by slaves who hoped to be freed, liberated the island and reclaimed Fort Saint-Louis. The fortress was abandoned after 1815 when the Treaty of Vienna put an end to English-French competition for Caribbean territory.

A Walking Tour of Grand Case

Grand Case (say *grawn caz*) is tiny and has one main road that runs for about a mile down the center of town. It's a picturesque Creole village with a fine beach and a number of excellent eateries. Most of the European-trained gourmet chefs are set up in authentic West Indies houses, while local cooks serve island specialties from open-air *lo-los* (snack shacks). The contrast creates a festive atmosphere.

See Where to Eat, page 133, for information on individual restaurants.

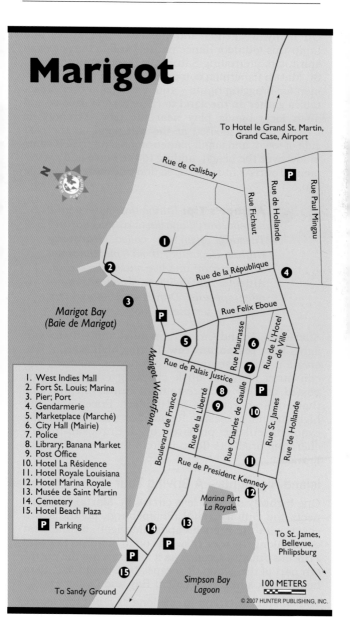

Marigot

Marigot Bay (Baie de Marigot)

Rue de Galisbay

Rue Fichaut

Rue de Hollande

Rue Paul Mingau

To Hotel le Grand St. Martin, Grand Case, Airport

P

Rue de la République

Rue Felix Eboue

Rue Maurasse

Rue de l'Hotel de Ville

Marigot Waterfront

Rue de Palais Justice

Boulevard de France

Rue de la Liberté

Rue Charles de Gaulle

Rue St. James

Rue de Hollande

P

Rue de President Kennedy

Marina Port La Royale

To St. James, Bellevue, Philipsburg

1. West Indies Mall
2. Fort St. Louis; Marina
3. Pier; Port
4. Gendarmerie
5. Marketplace (Marché)
6. City Hall (Mairie)
7. Police
8. Library; Banana Market
9. Post Office
10. Hotel La Résidence
11. Hotel Royale Louisiana
12. Hotel Marina Royale
13. Musée de Saint Martin
14. Cemetery
15. Hotel Beach Plaza

P Parking

To Sandy Ground

Simpson Bay Lagoon

100 METERS

© 2007 HUNTER PUBLISHING, INC.

On many weekends and holidays, boat races and jump-ups (outdoor dance parties) add to the convivial spirit. On alternating Saturdays throughout the year, St. Martin fishermen compete against Anguilla fishermen for bragging rights – and, perhaps, a beer. Spectators gather on the sand to cheer for the sailors, and often local bands play near the pier. Aéroport de L'Espérance is located at the salt pond on the east side of town, and small planes on final approach come in low over the beach, adding to the noise and excitement. Tourists fit right in, so don't hesitate to join the fun.

 Author's Tip: *During the winter tourist season, the village hosts a street party of Tuesday evenings called* **Harmony Nights***. Beginning about 6 pm, the street is blocked off and live music fills the air. Artists set out their work and restaurants offer specials. Drinks and snacks are sold from temporary kiosks.*

After dark, Grand Case grows quiet and glitters with lights from **restaurant row**. During high season, reservations are essential, but during the summer, you can stroll along at dusk checking out the menus posted outside each restaurant, until you find one that suits your tastes and budget. Prices are a bit high, but not excessive. Remember, you'll be enjoying exquisite cuisine prepared by a European-trained chef from products flown in from the US, Holland, or France.

Island Highlights – A Driving Tour

One highway more or less circles St. Martin and connects the Dutch capital (Philipsburg), on the south coast, with the French capital (Marigot), on the west coast. Along the way, it swings off to Simpson Bay and Princess Juliana Airport. As it loops across the northern part of the island, it scrapes by Grand Case, then heads back south past Orient Bay and Oyster Pond.

You can do the circuit in one long day, but this is one of the busiest highways in the Caribbean, so plan your route to avoid rush-hour traffic. Also, allow plenty of time for photo stops. The shore is lined with gorgeous bays, and the rolling countryside is sprinkled with flowers in flaming colors. Look for picturesque scenes at the following sites:

■ **Guana Bay**, off the secondary road that leads to the east coast from Great Salt Pond in Philipsburg. This is a high-end residential area with lovely homes set in the hills above the Atlantic.

■ **Falaise aux Oiseaux** (Cliff of the Birds), a steep ridge overlooking the Caribbean on the northern edge of Terres Basses (Low Lands), a small bit of ground that would be an island if it were not connected to St. Martin by thin ribbons of land that form the north and south shores of Simpson Bay Lagoon.

■ **Colombier**, northeast of Marigot, inland from Friars Bay, is named for the woodpigeons or doves that once inhabited this hilly area at the foot of Pic.

View from Pic Paradis

■ ★**Pic Paradis** (Paradise Peak), the island's highest point at 1,391 feet, offers awesome views. You can drive there on a steep, rutted road (off the main highway north of Marigot) that leads east through the village of Rambaud. Many cars can't make it, so be prepared to turn back if the going gets too rough..

■ You can also hike to the top on the **Sentier des Crêtes,** a strenuous trail that begins on the west end of Colombier. Once you're at the summit, you can see Marigot, Philipsburg, the entire coastline, and across the ocean to St. Barts, Tintamarre, and Anguilla.

■ **St. Louis**, off the main road south of Grand Case, is a small village above Friar's Bay that has majestic views of the western coastline.

■ **Anse Marcel**, reached by a secondary road off the main highway just past L'Espérance airport, northeast of Grand Case, is a secluded village in the hills along a lovely bay.

Worth a Visit

★**La Ferme des Papillons** (The Butterfly Farm). Don't miss this on the French side just north of the town of Orleans. It's a 3,000-square-foot mesh-enclosed garden with waterfalls and stocked fish  ponds. Hundreds of majestic butterflies from all over the world flutter freely to new-age music and land weightlessly on visitors' bodies. Try to visit when the doors first open in order to witness new babies being born and get in on the most active part of a butterfly's day. The $10 admission fee includes complimentary return visits, so make this stop early in your vacation. Take the guided tour to learn amazing facts and hear amusing stories about these gorgeous little creatures.

The farm, gift shop and snack bar are open daily 9 am-4:30 pm, with the last tour at 3:30. Look for the sign on the main highway as you approach Orient Beach.

Turn toward La Plage du Galion (Galion Beach), which is on Baie de l'Embouchure, north of Orleans, ☎ 590-87-31-21, www.thebutterflyfarm.com.

The St. Maarten Zoological & Botanical Park. If you're traveling with kids, or you happen to be an animal lover, make a visit to the zoo. It has a surprising number of unusual tropical animals, as well as lots of turtles and iguanas, and more than 180 parrots that fly freely throughout the three-acre park. One of the most interesting animals is the golden lion tamarin, a long-tailed monkey with a lion-like mane, which is one of the rarest endangered species in the world. Most of the animals are in open concrete enclosures with no fence. Birds are completely enclosed, but you can walk into the aviary cages.

St. Martin

Watch for yellow signs pointing the way to the zoo on Arch Road, north of Great Salt Pond, directly across from Philipsburg, in the residential area of Madame Estate. It's open daily, 10 am-6 pm in summer and 9 am-5 pm in winter. The entrance fee is $10 for adults, $5 for children two-12 years of age, and your ticket includes complimentary return visits. Stop by early in your vacation, then come back as often as you like to revisit your favorite animals. ☎ 599-543-2030, www.stmaartenpark.com.

Mount Vernon Plantation. This new park and museum near Orient Beach was once a working plantation. Now its shaded walking paths link historical buildings and period replicas scattered among tropical plants. French/English signs describe plantation life when sugar, coffee and cotton were important cash crops and an hour-long audio tour is included in the admission price. Look for the Plantation sign on the main road between Orient Bay and Grand Case. Open daily 9 am-5 pm. Tickets are priced at $14 for adults and $6 for children between the ages of two and 12. ☎ 590-29-50-62; www.plantationmontvernon.com.

★**Loterie Farm**. This 150-acre compound built in a dense secondary tropical forest is a step back in time, and you shouldn't miss the opportunity to visit. Many people come here to eat at the **Hidden Forest Café,** part of the restored 18th-century sugar plantation.

Loterie Farm (Jessica Payne)

Much of the fantastic food served in the open-air dining room is grown in the farm's garden. If you want to hike, a 1½-hour guided interpretive tour leaves on several mornings from the café. You can also explore on your own, and experienced hikers will want to go all the way to the top of Pic Paradis, the island's highest point. The newest feature at Loterie Farm is called "The Fly Zone," a zip-line treetop tour of the forest. Adults take a 1½-hour trip through 200-year-old tropical trees, while seated in a harness suspended on sturdy cables. Kids take the "Ti Tarzan" tour on swinging ropes.

The café is open Tuesday-Saturday, 11 am-3 pm and 6-11 pm, and on Sundays, 11 am-3 pm. You can hike the trails from sunup to sundown. Look for signs to the farm off the main highway between Marigot and Grand Case, which leads east through the village of Rambaud. Call for information about the guided hikes, which usually depart around 10 am on three or four mornings per week. ☎ 590-87-86-16, www. loteriefarm.net.

Old House. This museum is set up in a large Creole house at the top of a hill. It was once the great house of an 18th-century sugar plantation and is worth a visit when you're in the Orient Bay area. The garden

and house display tools and machines used in culti-
vating sugar cane and making rum, as well as interesting household objects from the plantation period.
Look for the giant *Old House* sign suspended high between two poles on the road between Orleans and Orient Bay. Admission is $5 for adults and $2.50 for
children under the age of 12. Open Tuesday-Sunday,
10 am-4 pm. ☎ 590-87-32-67.

Adventures on Water

Best Beaches

St. Martin has 36 beaches, about one for every square
mile of land. Those on the windward Atlantic side usually have more waves, unless they are in a protected
cove. The Caribbean beaches tend to be calmer. All
are open to the public, even those behind the guarded
gates of posh resorts. A few beaches can only be
reached via public-access trails that bypass the resorts.

★ Orient Bay Beach (Baie Orientale)

If you only visit one beach on St. Martin, make it Orient. Of course, you'll have plenty of company, but this
highly developed mile-long stretch of powdery white
sand is just too much fun to miss. The calm waters are
always filled with colorful Jet Skis, windsurfers and
Hobie Cats, and laughing kids run in and out of the
waves. Parasails glide overhead and gorgeously
bronzed bodies stroll the shore, browse at the open-air
boutiques, and loll on the beach. Tiki-hut snack bars
and full-service restaurants provide plenty to eat and
drink. On many days, local bands set up on the beach
to play original tunes and longtime island favorites
with a calypso beat.

 *You've probably heard about the nude
beaches on St. Martin. Actually, only one
is known for total nudity, Baie Orientale
(Orient Beach). At other French-side
beaches and pools, many women go topless, and you may see an occasional nat-*

uralist sunning au naturel. On the Dutch side, discreet topless sunbathing is tolerated, and one section of Cupecoy Beach is popular with nudists.

Club Orient Beach

Club Orient (☎ 590-87-33-85), at the south end of the crescent-shaped beach, is the famous nudist resort. Snorkeling conditions around the bay are good, with clear water most days. The protective coral reef just off the beach is teeming with critters.

Numerous bars and restaurants are open throughout the day and evening to provide a variety of food. Some are more like day resorts, with watersports, chair and umbrella rentals, massage huts, a boutique, and open-air showers or enclosed restrooms where you can dress before dinner.

Try ★**Bikini Beach Tapas Bar & Grill** (☎ 590-87-43-25) for a pricey but dependably good casual meal; **Boo Boo Jam** (☎ 590-66-17-99) for pizza and burgers, especially on Sundays, when the band plays; **Kontiki** (☎ 590-87-43-27) for grilled fish and sushi in a Polynesian setting; ★**Waikiki Beach** (☎ 590-87-43-19) for grilled freshly caught lobster; **Kakao Beach** (☎ 590-87-43-26) for pizza, steaks, and seafood; **Coco Beach** (☎ 590-87-34-62) for breakfast, fajitas, pasta, and frozen drinks. **Pirate** (no phone) has outstanding blender drinks served right to your lounge chair.

Hours vary from place to place, but you'll find something open from around 8 am until about 9 pm. Off-season, call ahead to check on closing hours if you want to have dinner, and be aware that some businesses close for several weeks during late summer. During peak season, phone for dinner reservations at the larger restaurants to guarantee a table.

From shore, you'll see the tiny isles of Green Cay, Tintamarre, and Pinel. You can take a water taxi from **Kontiki Watersports** (☎ 590-87-46-89) to Green Cay or Pinel for a day of snorkeling and sunning on the secluded beaches. Pinel has a restaurant, but Green Cay is deserted, except for day tourists.

Tiko Tiko, a luxury catamaran, sails to Tintamarre for an all-day beach party. Make arrangements through **Dolphin Watersports** (☎ 590-87-28-75) at Club Orient, and be aware that this is a clothing-optional event.

St. Martin

Cupecoy Bay Beach

Cupecoy Bay Beach

Located near the French-Dutch border that runs through Terres Basses (the Low Lands) just west of the airport, this beach is noted for its cliffs and caves. The water is too rough for children, so adults (including gays and nudists seeking privacy) enjoy plenty of laid-back peace and quiet. There are no watersports operations or bars, but you can rent an umbrella or pick up a snack from the guys who run a mobile operation on the north end of the beach.

Park in the lot next to the Cupecoy Beach sign and walk through the opening in the low wall to a path leading to the sand. Look for the picturesque **Cupecoy Boulder**, a big double-humped rock that juts from the sea. This marks the midway point, and you can walk either direction from there to find a good place to spread a towel. There's a steep drop-off and lots of rocks, which makes getting into the water a little tricky.

Mullet Bay

Maho & Mullet Bay Beaches

Located between the airport and Cupecoy Bay, these Dutch-side beaches are popular and often quite crowded, due to the nearby resorts, restaurants, casinos, and bars. You can walk from one beach to the other – they are similar, but different enough that each has its own fans. The star of Maho's shady rock-strewn beach is ★**The Sunset Beach Bar** (☎ 599-545-3998, www.sunsetbeachbar.com), a favorite happy-hour gathering place that roars with the sound of island music and 747 jet engines. Mullet has a mile-long beach with calmer water, but enough waves to be fun. Palms provide shade, making this a favorite spot for local families on weekends. The island's only golf course is nearby, but all the buildings are still closed due to hurricane damage several years ago, so the place has a rundown, almost spooky appearance.

St. Martin

Simpson Bay Beach

This crescent-shaped beach extends from the airport east to Pelican Key, but is one of the least visited on the island due to its location near the busy Airport Road. It's a great place to jog or stroll.

Great Bay Beach

Philipsburg's city beach is surprisingly nice. It's completely developed, with the shops, restaurants, and hotels facing inward toward Front Street. Fresh sand has been added recently and you can stroll the beach from one end of town to the other. Beach bars are set up right on the sand, and several restaurants offer patio seating overlooking the sea.

Great Bay Beach

Dawn Beach

Some of the island's best snorkeling and diving is on the easily accessible coral reefs just off lovely Dawn Beach. On a calm day, snorkel out from the center of the beach, cross over some dead coral, and begin looking for schools of fish and squid.

Bar on Dawn Beach

The beach is long, with white sand that meets the inlet to Oyster Pond at Babit Point on the north end. You can see St. Barts in the distance.

Look for the lumpy, bumpy road leading to Dawn Beach off the signed secondary road to Oyster Pond. Park at **Scavenger's Beach Bar**, ☎ 599-543-6155.

Oyster Pond isn't a pond at all, but rather a half-French, half-Dutch, shell-shaped bay that is almost completely surrounded by land. The French side is a well-developed yachting center and home to the popular **Captain Oliver's Marina** (☎ 590-87-33-47). Guests at **Captain Oliver's Hotel** (☎ 590-87-40-26) are water-taxied over to Dawn Beach for swimming, sunning, and snorkeling.

Oyster Pond

★Le Galion Beach

This beach on **Baie de l'Embouchure**, just south of
Orient Bay, is the island's best windsurfing beach.
Kids like it too because of the shallow, calm waters
near shore.

Windsurfing and kitesurfing rentals and lessons are
available.

Anse Marcel

A splendid 1,600-foot white sand beach lines this narrow cove cut deep into the northern shore. Some of the
island's poshest resorts are tucked into the 150-acre
nature preserve, along with **Port de Lonvilliers**, one
of the classiest marinas on the island. There are luxurious shops and exquisite restaurants, as well as a
cluster of French resorts. You'll find every amenity,
and if you wish to use them, speak to someone at the
activities desk or at the pool bar about paying a day-
use fee.

Anse Marcel

The jig-jag mountain roads between Anse Marcel and Cul de Sac, on the east coast north of Orient Bay, and Grand Case, on the west coast, are a thrill and offer panoramic views.

Grand Case

Almost as much fun as Orient Bay, but not nearly as nice, this town beach is lined with some of the island's best gourmet restaurants. On weekends and holidays, the residents have boat races, local bands play near the pier, and snack shacks (*lo-los*) serve up tasty West Indies dishes and grilled meats. The sand is narrow

Grand Case Beach

and slopes toward the water, so setting up a level lounge chair is a challenge. The water is calm and snorkeling is good.

Friar's Bay Beach

Friar's Bay Beach

This small protected stretch of sand is fairly quiet and uncrowded. Families and young locals show up on weekends to play volleyball and listen to boom-box music, and on full moon nights, locals and visitors to the island turn out for a party. Find the beach down a rough and winding road, off the main highway between Marigot and Grand Case.

An easy 10-minute walk to the north from Friar's Beach will bring you to **Happy Beach**, a secluded stretch of white sand strewn with black rocks and shaded by palms. There's no road to the beach, so only those in the know can find it. Bring your own eats and drinks.

Long Bay, Plum Bay, Red Bay

This trio of lovely beaches lines the north and west coasts of Terres Basses, south of Marigot. **Long Bay (Baie Longue)** is the longest stretch of beach on the island. The best section is near La Samana Resort. Other parts have rocks between the beach and water, making an ocean entrance difficult.

 *Plum Bay **(Baie aux Prunes)** has lovely dunes and soft sand that sprawls across the western edge of Terres*

Basses, giving it full afternoon sun. Since the beach is wild and undeveloped, with only a few houses beyond the dunes, this is an excellent spot for acquiring an all-over tan. You can walk there from Long Bay by rounding the point that juts out into the sea separating the two beaches. When conditions are right, surfers congregate at the north end to ride the waves near Falaises des Oiseaux (Bird Cliffs).

Baie Rouge sea grape

★**Red Bay (Baie Rouge)** is spectacular. Huge rocks that appear to be placed as decoration and abundant greenery add to the beauty. Unfortunately, tour buses stop here, so there's often a crowd, especially when cruise ships are docked in town. The water is calm and clear in most areas – ideal for snorkeling and swimming. Try to visit early in the day, before anyone else arrives. Get there on a signed road about a mile from Baie aux Prunes.

Simpson Bay Beach

Crescent-shaped Simpson Bay extends east from the airport to Pelican Key. The western end, called Simpson Bay Beach, has few visitors, probably due to its location near busy Airport Road. You may enjoy the privacy and find it a great place to jog or stroll.

Pelican Keys/Pelican Beach

Located at the far eastern end of Simpson Bay, Pelican Beach has a marina and a large watersports outfitter

(**Aqua Mania**, ☎ 599-544-2640), offering equipment rentals, scuba diving, and sailing excursions. The sand is protected by rock jetties at both ends, and you can use the free lounge chairs and umbrellas.

Seaside Solitude

If you want to find a rarely visited patch of sand for a solitary stroll or uninterrupted romance, try **Cay Bay**, at the foot of Cay Hill between Little Bay and Cole Bay. It's a favorite with horseback riders and hikers, but on most days no one's around. A small road off the main highway leads to Cay Bay, and you can follow the dirt horse path down to the beach. The water is calm and perfect for snorkeling.

Offshore islands are another option. From **Cul de Sac**, on the northeast coast, and nearby **Orient Bay**, you can get a water taxi to **Ilet Pinel**. Since it's fairly easy to get there, you'll probably have company, but you can get away by walking over the hill to the north shore. Unlike the south shore, which faces St. Martin and has gentle rolling waves,

Ilet Pinel

the north shore is battered by crashing surf. Don't plan to go into the water, but do stroll along the pebbly coast and explore the fascinating rock formations. Back on the south shore, you'll find a couple of Robinson Crusoe-type snack shacks and a watersports hut along the white sand beach.

 Kontiki Watersports, ☎ *590-87-46-89, at Orient Bay, will take you to Ilet Pinel for $15 and to Green Cay for $10 per person round-trip.*

Tintamarre

Tintamarre is a bit farther away and accessible by larger boats. If you want to go over for the day, check with the dive shops about scheduled trips. They may allow you to go along to snorkel, even if you don't scuba. Day charters to the island run about $80-$90 per person, including lunch, drinks, and snorkel equipment. You can also take a water taxi from Cul de Sac.

Tintamarre is 200 acres of deserted desert ringed by white sand beaches. As part of the marine reserve, the underwater world is teeming with fish and other sea animals.

NATURAL RESERVES

The entire coastline and everything under the water around Tintamarre is protected by the Réserve Naturelle de Saint-Martin and the Marine Park of Sint Maarten, which have been overseeing nature protection on the island since the early 1990s. This protection extends to the smaller islands of Tintamarre, Green Cay, and Pinel, as well as the reefs surrounding Creole rock. Boating and watersport activities are restricted in some areas, so check posted regulations at marinas and beach entrances.

Boardsurfing, Windsurfing & Kiteboarding

Kite surfing

You'll see people surfing off many of the island's beaches, but the best spot for both beginners and experienced wave riders is Orient Bay Beach. This two-mile stretch of white sand offers various conditions both inside and outside the protected bay. Dependable east and southeast trade winds create a good-to-excellent sailing environment year-round, with the strongest winds blowing from late November through March.

St. Martin

Orient's southern end is protected by a shallow reef and two nearby islands, Pinel and Green Cay, which guarantees smooth water on most days. A bit to the north, the conditions turn somewhat choppy and, outside the bay, Atlantic swells provide big thrills.

Expect to pay about $80 for a one-hour private windsurfing lesson, including equipment, and about $100 per day to rent a windsurf board. Kiteboarding lessons cost about $200 for a two-hour private lesson, including equipment. Surf boards and boards with kites rent for about $40 per hour. You'll need to prove that you know how to handle the equipment before you take it out. Package prices on lessons and rentals are substantially less per hour.

Wind Adventure

Orient Bay Resort

☎ 590-29-41-57, www.wind-adventures.com

Surf'ace
14 Rue du Général de Gaulle, Marigot

☎ 590-87-93-24, www.surf-ace-sxm.com

★Tropical Wave/Chez Pat
Le Galion Beach, Baie de l'Embouchure

☎ 590-87-37-25, fax 590-87-37-29, www.sxm-orientbeach.com/chezpat

 *The calm water of Simpson Bay Lagoon is ideal for **kayaking**. You can rent equipment or join a guided tour by contacting **Tri-Sports** (☎ 599-545-4384, www.trisportsxm.com) at 14 Airport Road in Simpson Bay. Paddle out to Great Key, a tiny island in the lagoon, for a picnic, or travel all the way across the water to Marigot or the resort beaches on Baie Nettlé.*

Sailing
St. Martin takes sailing seriously. Each March, the island hosts the **Heineken Regatta** (www.heinekenregatta.com), one of the largest and most exciting sailboat races in the Caribbean. The three-day

extravaganza draws more than 200 boats from over two dozen countries to races in 20 categories, from small catamarans to 50-foot vessels. Spectators follow the event as it progresses around the island. Parties follow each day's competition.

For more information, contact the Regatta Office at **Sint Maarten Yacht Club** in Philipsburg, ☎ 599-0544-2079, fax 599-544-2091, or visit the website at www.heinekenregatta.com.

For details about all of the island's regattas, contact the **Sint Maarten Yacht Club** on the Dutch side (see information above) or **Dockside Management** at Bobby's Marina in Philipsburg, ☎ 599-542-2366, fax 599-542-5442, www.bobbysmarina.com.

Charters

The following companies arrange both crewed and bareboat multi-day charters. Prices vary widely depending on the type of boat and length of charter.

The Moorings

Captain Oliver's, Oyster Pond

☎ 888-952-8420 (US), 590-87-32-55 (St. Martin), fax 590-87-32-54, www.moorings.com

Sunsail

Captain Oliver's, Oyster Pond

☎ 800-327-2276 (US), 250-758-5965 (Canada), 590-87-83-41 (St. Martin), fax 590-87-31-58, www.sunsail.com

Captain Alan's Boat Chaters

Great House Marina, Oyster Pond

☎ 599-524-1386, fax 599-580-6621, www.captainalan.com

Day-Sails

The highlight of your trip may well be a day-sail around St. Martin or to another nearby island. Most half-day cruise prices include snorkeling equipment and drinks, while longer sails include lunch or dinner, and, perhaps, time on a private beach.

You may be able to buy reduced-price tickets through the online seller **Saint Martin Activities**, ☎ 599-554-8715 or 599-580-2554, www.saint-martin-activities.com, or **Aqua Mania Adventures** at Pelican Marina, Simpson Bay, ☎ 599-544-2640 or 599-544-2631, www.stmaarten-activities.com.

Captain Morgan

Three-hour snorkeling trips run about $45 per person, full-day cruises are in the $75-$90 per person range, and a sunset dinner sail will cost about $66 per person. However, rates vary depending on the season, type of boat, destination, planned activities, and food service. Popular boats include:

Golden Eagle, Bobby's Marina, Philipsburg, ☎ 599-542-3323, www.sailingsxm.com. A variety of excursions includes one to Tintamarre, where you may relax, snorkel, and swim.

Captain Morgan, Port de Plaisance, Simpson Bay, ☎ 599-526-2467, www.captainmorgan-daycharters.com. Captain Serge sails this 65-foot schooner along both the Dutch and French coasts. Trips include open bar, snacks, lunch, snorkel gear and floats.

Lord Sheffield, Dock Maarten/Great Bay Marina, Philipsburg, ☎ 599- 552-0875, www.lordsheffield.com, offers a day of swimming, snorkeling and sunning. Equipment, lunch, and drinks are included.

White Octopus

St. Martin

White Octopus, Hot Tomatoes Pier, Simpson Bay, ☎ 599-557-9154, www.whiteoctopus.com. Look for this 70-foot motor-driven catamaran at the pier beside Hot Tomatoes Restaurant.

★*Random Wind*, Little Bay, ☎ 599-557-5742 or 599-544-5148, www.randomwind.com. This three masted 54-foot clipper offers a variety of excursions.

Scoobidoo, Anse Marcel and Grand Case, ☎ 590-52-02-53, www.scoobidoo.com. You may have seen this spiffy 75foot -catamaran on the Travel Channel. Take the sunset cruise, which features excellent appetizers and an open bar.

★Take the 12-Metre Challenge...

... if you think you're up to it. Whether you're a novice or an experienced sailor, you'll have a blast as a working member of the crew on one of the five 12-meter yachts that have competed in the America's Cup.

Allow half a day for this adventure. It begins with a pre-race briefing and ends with both winners and losers enjoying America's Cup – filled with Caribbean rum punch. Sign on for duty at **Bobby's Marina** in Philipsburg. ☎ 599-542-0045, www.12metre.com.

Motorboat Trips & Rentals

Sailboats are great, but sometimes you just want a little motor power. You can join a scheduled trip or rent
your own boat, with or without a skipper. Organized
group trips are priced about the same as sailboat
cruises, and boats rent for around $80 per hour with-
out a skipper, $90 with. If you rent for several hours or
a full day, you'll get a break on the hourly rates.

Aqua Mania Adventures

Pelican Marina, Simpson Bay

☎ 599-544-2640; www.stmaarten-activities.com

This outfitter offers motorboat excursions to nearby
islands for snorkeling and sunning on the beach.

Any Way Marine

Marina Port la Royale, Marigot

☎ 590-87-91-41, fax 590-29-34-76, www.
anywaymarine.com

Rent all kinds of boats at this outfitter, from a small
motorboat to a huge catamaran, for one-day or long-
term cruising.

Seaworld Explorer XI

This 49-foot semi-submarine allows you to stay comfortable and dry while you observe underwater reefs
and marine life through a large window. Only the ob-

servation level is submerged; the top of the ship remains above water at all times. Tickets are $39 for adults and $25 for children age two-12. For information and reservations, call **Atlantis Adventures**, ☎ 866-546-7820, 599-542-4078, www.atlantis-adventures.com.

Water Toys

Watersports operators are as abundant as beach bars on Orient Bay. You can stroll along the sand and view a colorful display of Jet Skis, Hobie Cats, and banana boats. Outfitters are less concentrated on other beaches around the island. Expect to pay about $55 per half-hour for a Jet Ski, $60 per 15-minute parasail ride, and about $52 per hour to rent a small Hobie Cat. Instruction and guided excursions are available and adapted to your skill level.

Orient Bay Beach

Club Orient Watersports, ☎ 800-690-0199 (US), 590-87-33-85, www.cluborient.com

Wind Adventures, ☎ 590-29-41-57, www.wind-adventures.com

Elsewhere on the Island

Aqua Mania Adventures, Pelican Beach, Simpson Bay, ☎ 599-544-2640, www.stmaarten-activities.com

Tropical Wave, Le Galion Beach, Baie de l'Embouchure, ☎ 590-87-37-25; www.sxm-orientbeach.com/chezpat

Blue Bubbles, Portofino Marina, Simpson Bay, and Oyster Pond Greathouse Marina, ☎ 599-554-2502, www.bluebubblessxm.com

Deep-Sea Fishing

Private charters cost from $350-$600 for a half-day and $650-$1,000 for a full day, depending on the boat and number of people in your party. Prices include all your gear and drinks, and usually some type of lunch on an all-day trip. The catch belongs to the captain, but most will clean, filet, and give you enough to cook for dinner. Join a scheduled group for about $250 per person per day.

Find a deep-sea fishing outfitter by strolling along the docks at any of the marinas. You can check out the boat, and possibly meet the captain before you sign on for a trip. The following fishing operators can be contacted by phone.

Rudy's Deep-Sea Fishing, Captain Rudy Sierens, Simpson Bay, ☎ 599-545-2177 (phone/fax) or 599-522-7120 (cell), www.rudysdeepseafishing.com

Lee's Deep-Sea Fishing, Airport Road, ☎ 599-544-4233, wwwleesfish.com.

Taylor Made Charters, Captain Dougie, Simpson Bay, ☎ 599-552-7539; www.stmartinstmaarten.com/taylormade

Adventures Underwater

Both the French and Dutch sides of St. Martin have a wide variety of dive sites, mostly off the west and south coasts. Count on lovely reefs with drop-offs, swim-throughs, and caves. Sunken wrecks, both accidental and deliberate, are plentiful and most are at depths of 40 to 60 feet. Some of the favorite sites are rock formations or dead coral reefs covered with new-growth sponges and corals.

The most famous of more than 40 official dive sites is the wreck of the English ship **HMS Proselyte**, which struck the reef and went down in Philipsburg's Great Bay in 1801. Divers can explore the remains of the 133-foot frigate and its coral-encrusted cannons and anchors. **Proselyte Reef**, on which the ship's remains rest, has elkhorn corals that are visited by groups of sergeant majors and yellowtail snappers.

The freighter **Teigland** was sunk deliberately on nearby **Cable Reef** in 1993, and vegetation growing on its

Elkhorn coral

hull has begun to attract a variety of fish, including schools of angelfish and an occasional eagle ray. Small caves within the reef formation harbor lobsters and eels. Nurse sharks and turtles also visit the area.

Most dive operators schedule trips to a basic list of 10 to 12 sites, and some go to locations off Saba, St. Eustatius, St. Barts, and Anguilla. If you aren't certified, check into a *Discover Scuba* introductory course that includes a shallow dive to about 30 feet. Also, most dive boats will allow snorkelers to go along if there's room. (If you want to snorkel on your own, the best spots are off Little Bay Beach, Dawn Beach, and Maho Bay Beach.)

Popular Dive Sites

Pelican Reef and **Molly Beday Island** are located in close proximity off the southeast coast around Oyster Pond. Molly juts about 100 feet above the surface of the water, and both have good coral formations. Lobsters live in crevices of the rocks, and shrimp and crabs dart among the coral.

Hens and Chickens (also called **Hens and Chicks**), southeast of Pointe Blanche Bay, is divided into a north and south area. The reef is alive with coral, sponges, and various sea plants. Visibility is usually good, but the site can be reached only when the ocean is calm. Rocks protrude above the waterline, and the reef has beautiful elkhorn forests at depths of 20 feet.

The reef descends to 70 feet, creating a wall that ends at the sandy bottom.

Creole Rock

Creole Rock, in Grand Case Bay, is ideal for novice divers and all snorkelers. There's a sandy bottom and plenty to see at shallow depths. The reef isn't in great shape, thanks to hurricanes, heavy boat traffic, and uncontrolled beginner kicking, but there are lots of fish and an occasional turtle. Several dive shop operators bring groups to the rock, and you can catch a boat ride from Grand Case Beach Club (contact the Activities Desk, ☎ 590-77-10-25) for about $35, including snorkeling gear.

French Reef, off the far south coast near Little Bay, is close to shore and has large numbers of fish at shallow depths; perfect for beginners. Snorkelers can enter the water off Little Bay Beach and view colorful tropical fish on the reef in 12 to 25 feet of water.

Tug Boat *Anny* stands upright on the sandy bottom of Simpson Bay. Fish have become accustomed to people and surround divers who descend to the 40-foot boat that's submerged in about 25 feet of water. This is a great place for underwater snapshots and night dives.

Fuh Sheng is a wrecked 120-foot fishing vessel from Taiwan. It's lying on its side on the sandy bottom of Cupecoy Bay at a depth of 110 feet. This is a favorite with experienced divers.

St. Martin

Shark Park

For something a bit different, consider going along with the folks at Dive Safaris to their shark park, a specially developed playground populated by about 20 reef and milk sharks. This isn't all about thrills. You'll also learn about the creatures and their life-style, with the hopes that you will appreciate their good qualities and spread the word that they're not re-ally such scary bad guys. By the time you descend among them, you should feel comfortable as well as awed.

The people who've developed this site are aware of all the potential problems, and they won't do anything to harm either sharks or humans. They limit feeding to around 20 pounds of food per week, or one pound per shark – not even a good-sized snack for an animal that devours the equivalent of 10% of its body weight per week. There's no danger that this small amount of food, offered piece-by-piece from the end of a long stick, will stop the sharks from hunting for meals.

Speak with Whitney Keogh at **Dive Safaris** for all the details, ☎ 599-542-9001; www.divestmaarten.com/shark_awareness_dive.htm.

Dive Operators

The following dive shops offer first-class instruction, multi-level certification, guided dive trips, and equipment rental. Most operators schedule two boat trips daily and arrange instruction courses to suit student needs.

With gear, you'll pay $55-$65 for a one-tank dive, $90-$100 for a two-tank dive, and about $80 for an introductory resort-course dive. Prices may vary with the season, and multiple-dive packages average less per dive.

Ocean Explorers is the oldest dive shop on the island. It's run by Dominique and LeRoy French. Contact them on Simpson Bay Beach, ☎ 599-544-5252, www.stmaartendiving.com.

Dive Safaris has two locations with well-stocked retail stores. In addition to shark dives, they specialize in equipment rentals, provide information on shore dives, and they are certified to guide handicapped divers. Dive Safaris, La Palapa Marina, Simpson Bay, ☎ 599-545 2401, fax 599-545 2429; Dive Safaris, Bobby's Marina, Philipsburg, ☎ 599-542 9001, fax 599-542 8983; www.divestmaarten.com.

Scuba Fun is located at the Port Lonvilliers Marina in Anse Marcel and Great Bay Marina, near the cruise-ship terminal. Specially outfitted boats take divers to a variety of sites. ☎ 590-87-36-13, 599-542-3966, fax 590-29-11-64, www.scubafun.com.

Neptune Dive Center, Orient Bay Beach, makes three 1½-hour dives per day. Their high-powered 22-foot boat allows them to get to great sites in 10 to 20 minutes, allowing a full 50 minutes underwater. Groups are small, up to six people, so everyone gets plenty of individual attention with no waiting-around time. ☎ 590-87-93-53, www.neptune-dive.com.

Most resorts have on-site dive facilities or affiliations with a nearby dive shop. Ask at the activities center or front desk for information, or call one of the dive operators listed above. Many will pick you up at your hotel.

St. Martin

Adventures on Land

Horseback Riding

Bayside Riding Club

Le Galion, Baie de l'Embouchure

☎ 590-87-36-64 or 599-557-6822, www.baysideridingclub.com

Choose from a one-hour ride along the beach ($70) or a two-hour ride and horseback swim ($95). Call the club, next to the Butterfly Farm across from the salt pond at Orient Bay, for reservations and information about riding lessons and departure times.

Lucky Stables

Cay Bay

☎ 599-544-5255

The friendly guides at Lucky Stables lead one- and two-hour treks ($60 and $85) through one of the last sparsely developed areas of the southern Dutch side.

If you have a specific spot you'd like to explore, just ask and a customized route will be mapped out for you. Wear your swimsuit. All rides end with a romp through the ocean astride your horse.

Hiking

Exploring St. Martin's countryside on foot is a terrific way to escape the traffic jams, beach crowds, and city shoppers. Hiking trails crisscross the island and lead to mountain-top vistas and coastal seclusion.

One of the most popular hikes is through **Loterie Farm** to the summit of **Pic Paradis** (Paradise Peak), the island's highest point. You can stroll the lush lower levels of the 150-acre farm's forest, or take the 2½-hour uphill trek to the peak. The view from the top is worth every sweaty minute. The latest adventure is The Flyline, a zipline through the trees. Look for signs to the farm off the main highway between Marigot and Grand Case, which leads east through the village of Rambaud, ☎ 590-87-86-16, www.loteriefarm.net.

You can also hike up Pic Paradis along the rutted trail that pretends to be a dirt access road, but it's really suitable only for four-wheel-drive vehicles. Find it off

the main road out of Marigot, going toward Colombier,
just past a road sign pointing the way to St. Louis.
Drive as far up the road as you wish (or as far as your
car can manage), then continue on foot. As you climb,
the vegetation becomes more lush, since more rain
falls at the higher elevation. When you get to the radio
tower at the top, you'll have unbeatable views of the
west coast. A little trail to the left of the fence enclos-
ing the tower (as you face it from the road) will take
you to a viewing point of the east coast and
Philipsburg, to the south. On a clear day, you may be
able to see St. Barts.

A group called **Action Nature** (Marigot, ☎ 590-87-97-
87) maintains a network of trails through the island's
countryside and leads organized hikes on weekends.
Call for a current schedule. Local hikers turn out for
the weekly excursions, and you're welcome to go
along, but you may prefer a private hike with a member of **AGRP (Association des Guides Randonneurs)**,
☎ 590-87-97-87, or **Dutch Hikers**, ☎ 599-548-3322.

Tri-Sports (☎ 599-545-4384; www.trisportssxm.
com), on Simpson Bay, also leads eco-adventure
hikes. They can put you on the right track for an independent hike or sign you up for a guided excursion
geared toward your experience and endurance level.
They also carry any type of sporting equipment you
may need, and know about road races and other
events scheduled on the island. You may want to just
drop by their store at 14 Airport Road to check out
what's going in, whether you're a sports spectator or
participant.

Mountain & Off-Road Biking

Don't bike along St. Martin's roadways. The streets
are narrow and there's too much traffic. However, off-
road biking is terrific. You can rent a bike, pick up
maps, and get route information from **Tri-Sport** in
Simpson Bay or **Frog Legs Bike Shop** in Marigot. The
staff can take you on guided tours along the popular
single-track mountain trails that run from the Dutch
to the French side of the island, or arrange to have
your bike delivered to your hotel or trail site.

St. Martin

Rates are about $25 per day or $100 per week to rent a 21-speed front-suspension mountain bike with a helmet, lock, and water bottle. Guided mountain bike tours are in the $40-per-person range.

Bike Rental

Tri-Sport, 14 Airport Road, Simpson Bay
Monday-Friday 9 am-6 pm, Saturday 10 am
☎ 599-545-4384, fax 599-545-4385

Frog Legs Bike Shop, 183 Rue de Hollande, Marigot
☎ 590-87-05-11, fax 590-87-25-54; www.sxm-game.com/mtb.html

Tennis

Many resorts, villas, and hotels on both sides of the island have tennis courts, and playing conditions are good except when the wind kicks up. Check with your travel agent or your resort for information about the availability of courts, condition of the facilities, equipment rental, and the possibilities for organized tournaments, lessons, or games with the staff pro.

If your resort doesn't have courts or the courts aren't lighted for night play, you can usually arrange to play for a fee at another resort nearby. In addition, you can contact the local tennis clubs about the possibility of renting a court or setting up a game with club members.

Tennis Club

American Tennis Academy, Cul de Sac, ☎ 590-690-382217; www.americantennisacademy.net

Golf

Unfortunately, St. Martin is not a golfing destination. Its only golf course, which was a good one, was attached to the Mullet Bay Resort, and that was destroyed by Hurricane Luis in 1995. The resort has still not reopened, and the government has been disputing with various developers for years about the future of the land.

However, the heavily damaged golf course is still playable, and much of its vegetation has recovered. The location is naturally beautiful, but the course probably will not be well cared for until the resort issue is settled and new owners come on board. Golfers will still appreciate the challenge, especially of the back nine and the lagoon water holes.

The course opens daily at 7 am, and the last tee-time is 1:30 pm. Fees are $108 per person for 18 holes and $62 per person for nine holes, including cart rental. Club rentals run $26. Phone in advance for a tee time, ☎ 599-545-2850, ext 1850. For a list of upcoming events, check the St. Maarten Golf Association website, www.stmaartengolf.com.

Shopping

Along with Charlotte Amalie on St. Thomas, Philipsburg is well known as a duty-free bargain paradise for shoppers. While some of the claims are overblown, you can find terrific buys on imported merchandise and local products. Since goods are free of import duty and local sales tax, and each citizen of the US can bring back up to $600 worth of duty-free goods (see *Returning Home*, page 23, for additional information), the final cost of many items is much less than if you'd bought them at home.

Loose gemstones, local arts and crafts, and porcelain figurines such as Lladro pieces recently have been granted additional exemptions, so you may now bring these items home without paying duty or counting them toward your total duty-free allowance.

Liquor, European china and crystal, and jewelry are some of the best buys. If you're serious about getting a good bargain on specific merchandise, check prices and quality in shops and discount outlets at home, so you'll come to St. Martin as an informed shopper. You're likely to save 30% on perfumes, luxury watches, European ready-to-wear clothing, and advanced-technology cameras. Local art and products that aren't available in your hometown make wonderful gifts and cherished souvenirs, so they are a bargain at any price.

St. Martin

🦜 *Most stores on the Dutch side are open Monday-Saturday, 9 am-6 pm. On the French side, stores open Monday-Saturday, 8:30 am-12:30 pm and 2-7 pm, with a mid-day break for déjeuner. Many shops extend their hours and also open on Sunday if a load of cruise-ship passengers is expected. During low season, hours of operation may be reduced, especially on days when no ship is in port. Some proprietors close for several weeks during late summer, board up their windows against hurricanes, and go off on a vacation of their own.*

Top Shops in Philipsburg

Park free near the police station on Walter Nesbeth Road. (Watch for signs pointing the way as you enter town.) Paid parking is available a block closer to Front Street at the corner of Peterson Street and Cannegieter Street, just south of the Government Building. Rates are $1 per hour up to $14 for a full day.

Open-air vendors set up near the paid parking lot and on Great Bay Beach. You can get some good deals on souvenirs and T-shirts from these local businessmen, but browse a bit before you start buying.

The majority of shops are lined up along Front Street, with storefronts facing inward on both sides of the road. Recent refurbishing has improved the curb appeal somewhat, but, for the most part, the stores look fairly weathered and shabby on the outside.

A conspicuous exception is **Old Street Mall,** a narrow brick-paved alley lined with two-story faux-Dutch buildings and potted palms. The stores here are some of the most exquisite, including **Oro de Sol** (jewelry, ☎ 599-542-8895), **Colombian Emeralds** (jewelry, ☎ 599-542-6410), **Dutch Delfts Blue Gallery** (Holland's famous porcelain and tile, ☎ 599-542-5204), and the wickedly delicious **Belgian Chocolate Shop**, ☎ 599-542-8863.

While it's impossible to describe or even list all the best buys and worthy stores along Philipsburg's Front Street, the following are our favorites for either good prices, great atmosphere, or unusual merchandise.

Jewelry

Joe's Jewelry International, 92 A Front Street, ☎ 599-543-7020, 866-978-5597 (toll-free), www.joesjewelry.com.

Artistic Jewelers, 61 Front Street, ☎ 599-542-3456, www.artisticjewelers.com.

If you're the type that likes to change the look of your jewelry every time you change clothes, check out this store's assortment of mix-and-match rings and bracelets that can be worn alone or stacked in various arrangements.

Majesty Jewelry, 46 Front Street, ☎ 99-542-2473, www.majesticjewelers.com.

This family-owned store is now run by the second generation, so you can trust them to be around and stand behind anything they sell. And they sell a wide variety of brand name watches, jewelry, and loose or set diamonds.

Cameras & Video Equipment

There's no shortage of electronic gear and cameras on St. Martin. If you have the tenacity to shop several stores and possess a talent for bargaining, you can get some extraordinary deals. Do a little research before you leave home, so you'll know what you're looking for and what it's worth. Once you're on the island, stop into a couple of stores to check availability and prices.

Then go back to your favorite with cash or credit card in hand to make a reasonable offer. Chances are you'll walk away with a super buy.

Both of the stores below are well-stocked with cameras, digital cameras, and video equipment, with brand names such as Nikon, Olympus, JVC, Bose, and Sony.

Boolchand's, 50 Front Street, ☎ 599-542-2245.

Shoppers have been going to Boolchand's since the 1930s for jewelry, watches, and loose diamonds, but the store also has a good selection of electronic, video, and camera equipment.

Caribbean Camera Center, 93 Front Street, ☎ 599-542-5259, www.chalanisxm.com.

The name just about says it all. If you know what you want, this is the place to compare prices. If you don't have a clue, ask one of the sales staff to run through the virtues of different brands and help you decide what will work best for you.

Perfume, Cosmetics & Skin Care Products

Lipstick, Polo Ralph Lauren Building, 31 Front Street, ☎ 599-542-6051.

Marigot, the main town on the French side, has three of these popular cosmetic shops, but if you're not going to that side of the island, stop by this boutique inside the Polo Ralph Lauren Building. Look for products by Calvin Klein, Cartier, Dior, Nina Ricci, Estee Lauder, and many brands that are difficult or impossible to find in North America.

Liquor

Guavaberry Emporium, 8-10 Front Street, ☎ 599-542-2965, www.guavaberry.com.

Guavaberry liqueur is made on St. Martin, and sold throughout the islands. You can taste the liqueurs made with this local fruit at the Emporium housed in a colorful 18th-century building that stands on Front Street. If you like the sample, order a Guavaberry Colada to sip as you browse through the shop's other island-made products.

Gift World, 21 and 45 Front Street, ☎ 599-542-0338, www.giftworldddutyfree.com.

If you want to swoop up all your souvenirs, liquor, and gifts in one shop so that you can hit the beach before noon, this is the store for you. In addition to all the popular brands of liquor, the shelves are filled with sunglasses, T-shirts, post cards, and locally made crafts.

Philipsburg Liquor Store, Point Blanche Cruise Ship Port, ☎ 599-542-3587.

More than 1,000 types of wine and liquor are stocked here, so you're sure to find your favorites. Look for the colorful building located beside the cruise ship dock.

> *If you're leaving the island by plane, buy your liquor in the airport terminal from* ***Antillean Liquors****, ☎ 599-545-4267.*

Art

Greenwith Gallery, 33 Front Street, ☎ 599-542-4120.

Possibly the most beautiful shop on the island, Greenwith displays the works of more than 40 Caribbean artists. Choose original paintings, prints, or posters; everything may be purchased framed or unframed. The staff are experts at packing and will even bundle up delicate pottery for the trip back home.

Mosera, 7 Front Street, ☎ 599-542-0554.

Ras Mosera, a Rasta painter from Saint Lucia, creates and displays his oversized oil and watercolor paintings at this combination studio/gallery.

Tablecloths

Linen Galore, 97 Front Street, ☎ 599-542-2533.

Stock up on tablecloths, place mats, napkins, pillowcases, and other home accessories at one of these two linen boutiques. Choose from Battenburg Lace, embroidered, and crocheted items.

Island-Style Clothing & Stuff

Shipwreck Shop, 42 Front Street, ☎ 599-542-2962, www.shipwreckshops.com.

In addition to T-shirts and beach accessories, you'll find island-made arts and crafts, hammocks, spices, and baskets. Everything is well-priced, so load up that shopping bag.

Endless Summer, 27 Front Street, ☎ 599-542-1510.

In a perfect world, summer would last year-round, and you'd be dressed for the beach in the gorgeous designer swim wear and coverups sold here. Look for the stylish creations of Gottex, Pilpel, Anne Cole, Calvin Klein, Tara Grinna, and others. Ask the sales people to show you how to tie one of the colorful pareos into a Tahitian-style dress or skirt. A second shop is on Airport Road in Simpson Bay, ☎ 599-545-2618.

Dalila Boutique, 106 Old Street, ☎ 599-542-4623.

You won't be able to resist the exotic, made-in-Bali batik clothing and handicrafts sold at this small shop.

Del Sol, 23 Front Street, ☎ 599-542-8784.

Ah, technology is terrific. All the casual clothing at this store appears to be decorated with black-and-white designs, but when the fabric is exposed to the sun, the design comes alive with tropical colors. Step back inside, and the picture reverts back to black-and-white.

Rima Beach World, 95 Pond Fill Road (also called Nisbet Road), ☎ 599-542-1424, www.beachwearima.com.

As both a wholesaler and retailer, this factory outlet can offer fantastic prices. It's not on the main drag in Philipsburg, but across from the Heineken Bar (it looks like an airplane) on the road that runs parallel to the salt pond. The store has hundreds of swimsuits, coverups, shirts, towels, and beach bags.

Upscale Clothing & Accessories

The stores listed below sell the clothing and accessories designed by their famous designer namesakes. If you buy these brands at home, you'll recognize the bargains when you see them. Expect to save about 20% over prices in North America; more if you happen to find a sale.

This & That

New Amsterdam Store, 66 Front Street, ☎ 599-542-2787.

This three-level store near the courthouse on Wathey Square has been selling everything from designer shoes to fine china since 1925. Other shops along Front Street sell similar merchandise, but this one-stop outfit puts it all under one roof at competitive prices.

Ashburry's, 79 Front Street, ☎ 599-542-0832.

Only the best is displayed here. Fine leather luggage, exquisite sunglasses, pricey perfume, and fabulous jewelry are all laid out in this pleasant boutique. Plan to spend some time admiring, and perhaps coveting.

 Author's tip: *Le Grand Marché, 79 Bush Road, ☎ 599-542-4400, is the largest supermarket on the island. They carry a good selection of spices, sauces and liquor, as well as an abundance of produce and fresh foods.*

Best Boutiques in Marigot

In the French capital, shops are spread out among several streets, with the majority of fine boutiques on **Rue de la République** and **Rue de la Liberté**. You'll discover other great buys in stores along **Rue du Président Kennedy,** which borders the Marina Port la Royale, and scattered among the side streets. Vendors set up along the harbor, and a large **public market**

St. Martin

takes place at the waterside town square on Wednesdays and Saturdays. If you just want to pick up picnic supplies, sun block, or other everyday necessities, stop at **Match**, the French hypermart, on Rue de Hollande on the far northeast side of town, in the direction of Grand Case.

Park free in front of the Office du Tourisme (☎ 87-57-21) on Rue du Morne, the road leading into town from Sandy Ground to the south, or in the waterfront lot on Blvd. de France. The office has maps and a table with leaflets offering discounts at stores and attractions on the French side.

While Philipsburg is my choice shopping town for bargains on jewelry and Caribbean-style clothes and accessories, Marigot is generally better for European fashions, leather goods, and anything French. Here's a listing of my favorite shops based on merchandise selection, bargain prices, and friendly service:

Most of the stores in Marigot do not display a street number, but the roads are only a few blocks long, so you're never far away. Just stroll until you spot the sign or awning baring the store's name.

Jewelry

Oro de Sol, Rue de la République, ☎ 590-87-56-51.

If you know and love fine things, you'll be impressed with this shop's inventory of imported china, crystal, linens, designer jewelry, and top-name watches.

Chopard, 26 Rue de la République, ☎ 590-51-01-15.

There are those among us who wear only Chopard, the Swiss name made famous in 1860. All others should strive for such heights of luxury. The watches, of course, are absolute perfection, but many are not aware of the excellent Chopard collections of silk scarves and ties, silverware, perfumes, sunglasses, and jewelry. Come. Look. Admire.

Passions, Port la Royal, ☎ 590-87-18-00.
Search out a little bauble at this upscale jewelry shop. The collection includes watches by Jaeger-Lecoultre, Chanel, Bell & Ross, Girard-Perregaux, and Chaumet. Unique jewelry designs are by Dinh Van, Pomellato, Hermès, and O.J. Perrin. Browse the luxury, even if you don't buy.

Liquor & Wine

(See sister-store reviews for Vinissimo and Le Goût du Vin under *Top Shops* in the St. Barts section.)

Vinissimo, 1 Rue Low Town, ☎ 590-87-70-78

Designer Sunglasses

Optical, Rue du Général de Gaulle, ☎ 590-87-13-08

Optic 2000, 3 Rue du Président Kennedy, ☎ 590-52-97-82

> *Don't dismiss **Little Switzerland** on Rue de la République (☎ 590-87-50-03) as a been-there-seen-it-all place. The one in Marigot carries additional French merchandise.*

European Fashions & Accessories

Serge Blanco, Rue du Président Kennedy/Marina Port la Royale, ☎ 590-29-65-49.
Named for one of the most talented rugby players in history, this shop carries men's shirts, shorts, and jackets made near Blanco's hometown of Biarritz, France.

Act III, Rue du Général de Gaulle #3, ☎ 590-29-28-43.
Shop here for the perfect evening gown or cocktail dress. The exquisite fashions carry labels such as Thierry Mugler, Christian Lacroix, and Cerruti.

Max Mara, 6 Rue du Président Kennedy, ☎ 590-52-99-75.
Italians can't get enough of the fashions found at Max Mara, and you'll understand why when you see the easy-to-wear designs made of top-quality fabrics.

St. Martin

Perfume, Cosmetics & Skin Care Products

Lipstick, Rue du Président Kennedy/Marina Port la Royale, ☎ 590-87-73-24

Without question, this is the best shop on the island for skin care products, cosmetics, and perfume. You'll find all your old favorites and discover the latest beauty products from Europe. The Marina Port la Royale location also has a full-service salon.

Cameras & Video Equipment

Maneks, Rue de la République, ☎ 590-87-54-91.

Name-brand cameras, such as Nikon, Pentax, and Canon, share space with Swiss Army knives, designer T-shirts, and Cuban cigars at this one-stop shop.

This & That

L'Epicerie, Marina Port la Royale, ☎ 590-87-17-69.

L'Epicerie means *the grocer's shop* in French, but don't mistake this elite little market for a common neighborhood food store. Yachtsmen and residents come here to stock their kitchens with imported caviar, foie gras, truffles, smoked salmon, chocolates, and fine wines, vodkas, and champagnes. Stop in to pick up fancy treats for a romantic picnic on the beach or a party back at your villa.

Where to Stay

Private Villas

While private rentals are less common on St. Martin than on St. Barts, some fabulous properties and a few simple cottages are available through individual owners and various agencies. Be sure to browse the Internet for homes, apartments, timeshare units, and bungalows offered by individuals, but shop carefully and be aware that what's advertised is not always what you get. If the price seems too low, you're probably looking at an undesirable location or a rundown shack.

Telephoning

Calling to, from, or within St. Martin is confusing. When calling St. Martin from the US or Canada, dial **011** to get international service, then the area code, **590** for the French side and **599** for the Dutch side, plus the on-island number, which will be seven digits on the Dutch side (example: 011-599-xxx-xxxx) and nine digits on the French side, which means dialing 590 twice (011-590-590-xx-xx-xx).

When calling the island from Great Britain, dial **00** to get international service, then the area code, **590** or **599**, plus the on-island number, which means you will dial 590 twice to reach the French side (00-590-590-xx-xx-xx).

To call within the French territory, you must add a **0** to the nine-digit local number (0590-xx-xx-xx).

When calling a French number from Dutch St. Martin, dial 00, then 590, then 590 again, plus the six-digit number (00-590-590-xx-xx-xx).

If you wish to call Dutch St. Martin from the French side, you must dial 1 + 599 + the seven-digit number. To call Dutch St. Martin from St. Barts, dial 00, then 599 plus the seven-digit local number.

RENTAL AGENCIES	
WIMCO	☎ 800-449-1553, www.wimco.com
Villa Lady	☎ 800-338-4552 (in the US), www.villalady.com
French Caribbean International	☎ 800-322-2223, www.frenchcaribbean.com
Jennifer's Vacation Villas	☎ 599-544-3107, fax 599-544-3375, www.jennifersvacationvillas.com

St. Martin

Resorts & Hotels

Whether you prefer a sumptuous Dutch high-rise with its own casino or a small French compound with plenty of solitude, look for a package deal which may in-

HOTEL PRICE CHART	
For a double room for two	
$	under $300
$$	$300-$400
$$$	$401-$550
$$$$	over $550

clude airfare, rental car, or discounts at restaurants and watersports centers.

Tour-scan computerizes published package trips to the Caribbean according to season, then selects the best values for each island. You can search for your vacation by destination, cost, hotel rating, and preferred activity. ☎ 800-962-2080, www.tourscan.com.

We've checked out a variety of accommodations to come up with the following list of recommendations. At one time, travel professionals advised "staying on the Dutch side, but playing on the French side." Then, the sages began to advocate staying on the quieter French side, but playing on the livelier Dutch side. We tried both, and can frankly tell you it doesn't matter. The differences between the two sides have become as indistinct as the border that divides them.

The above scale indicates rates charged per night for a standard double room for two adults during high season. All prices are given in US dollars. A government tax of 8% and a 10-15% service charge will be added to the cost of your room, but may be hidden in the quoted rate. Be sure to ask.

 All recommended resorts and hotels are air conditioned, meet average expectations for comfortable furnishings, and are equipped with color cable TV.

Accommodations Directory

THE DUTCH SIDE
Atrium Resort, Simpson Bay, ☎ 599-544-2126, fax 599-544-2128, $$
Belair Beach Resort, ☎ 800-480-8555 (US), 599-542-3366, fax 599-542-6017, www.belairbeach.com, $$$
Caravanserai Beach Resort, Burgeaux Bay, ☎ 800-616-1154 (in the US), 599-545-4000, fax 599-545-540, $$
Divi Little Bay Beach Resort, Little Bay, ☎ 800-367-3484 (in the US) or 599-542-2333, fax 599-542-5410, $$$
Holland House Beach Hotel, Philipsburg, ☎ 800-223-9815 (in the US) or 599-542-2572, fax 599-542-4673, $$$
The Horny Toad Guesthouse, Simpson Bay, ☎ 800-417-9361 (in the US) or 599-545-4323, fax 599-545-3316 **RATE?
La Vista Resort, Pelican Key, ☎ 599-544-3005, fax 599-544-3010**RATE?
Mary's Boon Beach Plantation, Simpson Bay, ☎ 599-545-4235, fax 599-545-3403, $
The Ocean Club, Cupecoy Beach, ☎ 800-942-6725 or 599-545-4362, fax 599-545-4434, $$$
Pasanggrahan Royal Guest House, Philipsburg, ☎ 599-542-3588, fax 599-542-2885, www.pasanhotel.com, $
Sapphire Beach Club, Cupecoy Beach, ☎ 599-545-2179, fax 599-545-2178, $$$
Sonesta Maho Beach Hotel and Casino, Maho Bay, ☎ 800-223–0757 (in the US) or ☎ 99-545-2115, fax 599-545-3180, $$

St. Martin

On the Dutch Side

★★Caravanserai Beach Resort

Burgeaux Bay

☎ 877-796-1002 or 866-786-2278 (in the US), 599-545-4000, fax 419-781-7694
www.caravanseraibeachresort.com

66 units

$$

Set beside a small beach near Maho Beach and the airport, the Caravanserai just keeps getting better. The resort includes one-bedroom apartment-style ocean-view suites, in addition to spacious hotel rooms. On-site attractions include the **Dolphin Casino**, **Bamboo Bernie's Restaurant**, **Bliss** (a nightclub, restaurant, and martini bar), and the popular **Sunset Beach**

Bar. A small Asian grocery store/café has a few tables and offers Chinese food to go. The landscaped grounds encompass four swimming pools, two tennis courts, a health spa and duty-free shops.

★★Divi Little Bay Beach Resort)

Little Bay

☎ 800-367-3484 (in the US) or 599-542-2333, fax 599-542-4336

www.divilittlebay.com

245 units

$$$

AUTHOR'S PICK
LARGE RESORT

The beach sand has been refreshed, and Little Bay is a great location; the site of Fort Amsterdam. It sits on a peninsula that juts into the sea southwest of Philipsburg, and the views are fantastic. Sprawled across several landscaped acres, the rooms and suites are in colorful Dutch-colonial buildings clustered around three pools, two tennis courts, three restaurants, and a well-equipped watersports/dive shop facility. Many of the units have little kitchens and spacious bathrooms with whirlpool tubs and showers. There are scheduled activities, including a weekly barbecue with live music.

★★Atrium Resort

Simpson Bay

☎ 599-544-2126, 866-933-7848 (toll-free US), fax 599-544-2128, www.atrium-resort.com

90 studio, one- , two- , and three-bedroom units

$$$

AUTHOR'S PICK
SMALL RESORT

Spacious units in this high-rise have full kitchens and wide balconies with views of the Caribbean. Ceiling fans and tiled floors

St. Martin

add a touch of island chic, and a decked pool area is a nice complement to the resort's long white-sand beach. Amenities are scarce, but a restaurant is located near the pool, and you'll be within walking distance of the eateries and shops along Airport Road. The popular Buccaneer Bar is on the beachand open daily for lunch, dinner and late-night drinks.

Wyndham Sapphire Beach Club

Cupecoy Beach

☎ 877-231-8767 (US & Canada), 599-545-2179, fax 599-545-2178, www.sbcwi.com

180 studio, one- and two-bedroom units

$$

We think this Wyndham resort is a good value on the Dutch side. Even the smallest units have full kitchens with granite countertops and dishwashers, bedrooms with king-size beds and a terrace, a living room with a sleeper sofa, VCR, and Italian marble bathrooms with big tubs. All for less than $100 per person per night during high season. Unlike some timeshare properties, this one has daily maid service, except on Sundays.

Sonesta Maho Beach Hotel and Casino

Maho Bay

☎ 800-766-3782 (US & Canada) or ☎ 599-545-2115, fax 599-545-3180, www.sonesta.com/mahobeach

600 rooms and suites

$$$

This is by far the largest hotel complex on the island, and one of the best known in the Caribbean. Guests get lost in the twists and turns of the walkways that connect their room to the casino (the largest on the island), nine restaurants, two pools (one is the largest on the island), nightclub, spa, gym, three bars, four tennis courts, about 40 boutiques, and lovely Maho Beach. But no one minds – it's just too much fun. The only drawback is the darn jumbo jets that fly directly overhead. (Rooms are soundproofed.) Units in two high-rise towers aren't spectacular, but they're fairly spacious and have some nice touches, such as new furnishings, Italian tile, and bidets in the bathrooms. Check out the services of **The Good Life Spa** at www.the goodlifespa.com.

★★ Mary's Boon Beach Plantation

Simpson Bay

☎ 599-545-7000, fax 599-545-3403, www. marysboon.com

25 rooms, studios, and one- or two-bedroom apartments

$$

AUTHOR'S PICK SMALL HOTEL This is a personal favorite – a quiet, well-run inn on three miles of white-sand beach. Owners Mark and Karla Cleveland keep everything running smoothly so guests do nothing but relax. Smaller units have kitchenettes, and the one- and two-bedroom bungalows have full kitchens – perfect for keeping picnic supplies on hand. Ask about the new deluxe studios with four-poster king-size beds and verandahs that face the sea.

A swim-up bar has been added to the lovely pool and Jacuzzi. Watersports are available on the beach for

the energetic, and there are spa services for those who wish to be pampered. The **Tide Restaurant & Bar** serves a delicious fixed-price, family-style West Indies meal and à-la-carte choices every evening, which shouldn't be missed. On Sundays, chef Leona features a superb Champagne Brunch. Reservations are a must.

La Vista Resort and La Vista Beach Resort

Pelican Key

☎ 599-544-3005, 888-790-5264, fax 599-544-3010, www.lavistaresort.com

32 suites and cottages

$$

Along with your room at this charming inn, you get full privileges at the tennis courts, watersports center, and spa that belong to neighboring Pelican Resort and Casino.

Every unit, from the junior suite to the oversized one-bedroom penthouse, has a king-size bed, either a patio or balcony, and a kitchenette.

La Vista Beach Resort is across the street and sits directly on the beach. If you book one of these newer rooms, you'll have a fabulous view of the sunset from your balcony. Each of the 18 units has a small fully-equipped kitchen and ceiling fans in addition to air conditioning. The studios have a sitting area that can provide added sleeping room for children. Two-bedroom units have two full bathrooms, a king-size bed in the master bedroom and two twin-size beds in the second bedroom. Outside, a new waterfront swimming pool is surrounded by a large furnished deck.

The Horny Toad Guesthouse

Simpson Bay

☎ 800-417-9361 (in the US) or 599-545-4323, fax 599-545-3316

www.thehornytoadguesthouse.com

Eight units

$$

After an initial quick glance, we dismissed this inn as too simple to make the recommended list. And, honestly, we were surprised by the rate, $198 per couple per night during the winter, which we thought was too high. Still, we had heard good things about the friendly laid-back mood promoted by owner Betty Vaughan and the fanatic attention to detail of the cleaning staff, so we poked around a bit. Now, we're happy to report a complete change of attitude. Who needs air conditioning, swimming pools, and on-site restaurants when you can have soft breezes straight off the beach and cook your own dinner on a communal gas barbecue grill set up in a covered seaside pavilion?

This place isn't for everyone, and kids younger than seven are not welcome, but each individually decorated unit in the converted beach house (built in the 1950s by a former governor) is comfortably homey. The beds are king size; the bathrooms are basic, but sparkling; the kitchens are equipped with everything you need, including a full-size refrigerator; and the grounds are landscaped with fragrant flowering bushes. If you think you can't make do with only a ceiling fan, request one of the air-conditioned units.

Holland House Beach Hotel

Philipsburg

☎ 800-223-9815 (in the US) or 599-542-2572, fax 599-542-4673
www.hhbh.com

60 rooms and suites

$$

If you're going to stay in the Dutch capital – and we don't recommend it unless you're on a business or serious shopping trip – check into the Holland House. One side faces Front Street, lined with duty-free shops, and the other faces Great Bay Beach, lined with lounge chairs shaded by yellow umbrellas. The lobby has an old-world appearance with buffed hardwood floors, but the hotel offers modern high-speed Internet access to guests.

Ask for a room facing the water, and request a kitchenette if you want to keep drinks and snacks on hand. Each room is spacious and has a balcony, but the bathrooms are small. Even if you don't stay in the hotel, enjoy fine dining or drink at the recently renovated **Ocean Lounge**.

The Ocean Clubs

Cupecoy Beach

☎ 599-545-4362, fax 599-545-4434
www.oceansnclubs.com

50 villas and suites

$$$

We liked this stunning white village because of its high level of luxury, the gorgeous location, and, most of all, the relaxed atmosphere. Instead of non-stop activities, the resort offers convenient access to one of the island's most popular beaches, a private 45-foot diesel-powered

yacht that cruises the shoreline and lagoon, a large free-form swimming pool, and a very good restaurant, The Oasis. A one-week diet, fitness and massage program is offered at the club for guests of the resort.

Belair Beach Resort

Little Bay Beach

☎ 599-542-3366, fax 599-542-6017, www.belairbeach.com

72 one- and two-bedroom suites

$$$

Attention all beach bums: This place is for you. The door to your suite will open directly onto the sandy beach at Little Bay, which is a short distance west of Great Bay in Philipsburg.

The resort itself is showing some signs of age and could use a bit of upgrading here and there, but everything is clean, the staff is friendly and the on-site **Gingerbread Café** serves meals and drinks all day. Each unit has a well-equipped kitchen, dining/living area with a sleeper sofa and a private patio or balcony.

Since the resort is also a timeshare, you'll have the benefit of a well-run activities desk and waterside sports center as well as use of the on-site coin-operated laundry, freshwater pool and tennis court.

Pasanggrahan Royal Guest House

Front Street, Philipsburg

☎ 599-542-3588, fax 599-542-2885, www.pasanhotel.com

30 rooms

$$

Ask for the **Queen's Room** when you book accommodations at this in-town hotel that was originally the home of the island's Dutch governor. The queen never slept there, but it's the best room in the house and has a private balcony. When the Netherlands' Queen Wilhelmina and Princess Juliana visited Sint Maarten, they stayed on the lower floor in what has been converted into the **Sydney Greenstreet Bar**.

If royalty doesn't impress you, maybe the hotel's location will. It's tucked into a shady tropical garden on the beach at the edge of the capital city. Businesspeople love it, but it's also popular with newlyweds looking for quaint romance and anyone who wants to be within walking distance of shops, casinos, piers and restaurants in Philipsburg. Afternoon tea is a bonus.

THE FRENCH SIDE

Captain Oliver's Resort, Oyster Pond, ☎ 590-87-40-26, fax 590-87-40-84, $$

Caribbean Princess Condos, Orient Bay, ☎ 590-52-94-94, $$$$

Club Orient Resort, Orient Bay, ☎ 590-87-33-85, fax 590-87-33-76, $$$$

Grand Case Beach Club, Grand Case, ☎ 590-87-51-87, fax 590-87-59-93, $$$$

Green Cay Village, Orient Bay, ☎ 888-843-4760 (in the US) or 590-87-38-63, fax 590-87-39-27 **RATE?

Hotel Beach Plaza, Marigot Bay, ☎ 590-87-87-00, fax 590-87-18-87, www.hotelbeachplazasxm.com, $$$

La Samanna, Baie Longue, ☎ 800/854-2252 or 590-87-64-00, fax 590-87-87-86, $$$$

L'Esplanade Caraïbes Hotel, Grand Case, ☎ 590-87-06-55, fax 590-87-29-15, $$$$

Le Petit Hotel, Grand Case, ☎ 590-29-09-65, fax 590-87-09-19, $$$

The Mercure Simpson Beach, Baie Nettlé, ☎ 590-87-54-54, fax 590-87-92-11, $$$

Orient Bay Hotel, Orient Bay, ☎ 800-818-5992 (in the US) or 590-87-31-10, fax 590-87-37-66, $$$

Palm Court, Orient Bay, ☎ 866-786-2277 (toll-free in the US) or 590-87-41-94, fax 590-29-41-30, $$$$

St. Tropez des Caraïbes Beach Club, Orient Bay, ☎ 590-87-42-01, fax 590-87-41-69, www.st-tropez-caraibes.com, $$

St. Martin

★★La Samanna

Baie Longue
☎ 800/854-2252 or 590-87-64-00, fax 590-87-87-86
www.lasamanna.com
83 rooms and suites; four star deluxe

$$$$

AUTHOR'S
PICK
LARGE
RESORT
★

In spite of its reputation as the standard by which all other luxury resorts measure themselves, La Samanna is surprisingly

easygoing. The resort puts as much thought and money into making you feel relaxed and pampered as it puts into impressing you with Asian objets d'art and exquisite Indonesian furniture made of fine mahogany and teak.

The new spa is rated one of the best in the Caribbean and features environmentally serene massage rooms and two hydro-therapy areas where European-trained therapists perform a variety of services using highly effective natural products from France. A new air-conditioned fitness pavilion allows you to gaze at the sea while you work out on Cybex machines under the direction of certified instructors, and the cardio equipment has individual TVs.

After dark, torches light the new floating-edge swimming pool, which seems to overflow toward the sea. Be sure to wear a large pair of dark sunglasses when you lounge here during the day so you can covertly spy on big-name celebrities hiding under nearby umbrellas.

The bathrooms are huge and sumptuous, and the TVs and VCRs are cleverly hidden away in lovely benches when not in use, then pop up in an instant when you want them.

A run down on the amenities reads like a tropical dream: 55 acres of gardens shaded by towering palms set on more than a mile of sandy beach; a gourmet French restaurant serving savory cuisine by candlelight on a lovely patio overlooking the water; watersports for daytime diversion and a disco for dancing the night away. If you're celebrating a special occasion, book the new 1,200-square-foot **Romance Suite**, which has a private plunge pool and is stocked with love-themed DVDs, CDs and novels.

Palm Court

Orient Bay

☎ 590-87-41-94, fax 590-29-41-30

24 rooms

$$$$

Palm Court is especially popular with watersports enthusiasts because it's just steps from the beach, scuba shops, and watersports centers. Actually, it's a good choice for anyone who wants to be near all the restaurants, shops and activities on Orient

Bay. This all-suite resort was recently renovated with exotic Moroccan décor, mood lighting and elegant furnishings. Each suite has a dining/living area and is outfitted with a microwave, small stove, and a fridge. Every room has either a king-size bed or two double beds, an ample bathroom, and fans as well as air conditioning. Deluxe rooms on the second floor are particularly pleasant because of their high-beamed ceilings and ocean-view balconies. Ground-floor rooms open onto the lush garden-like grounds, which feature a swimming pool and are shaded by palm and fruit trees.

Club Orient Resort
Orient Bay
☎ 800-690-0199, 590-87-33-85, fax 590-87-33-76, www. cluborient.com
136 rooms and bungalows
$$$

If you're not accustomed to going about buck naked, this place will take some getting used to. It's called *clothing optional,* but everyone takes the unclothed option rather than look like an out-of-place duffus.

Once you get past the clothing issue, the resort is fairly typical. It sits on high-priced real estate near the water on the powdery white sand lining Orient Bay. Each unit features a kitchen, ceiling fans in addition to air conditioning, and an outdoor shower as well as a full bathroom. Furnishings are comfortable, but rather plain, and there are no TVs or telephones in the rooms. A fully clothed maid cleans daily.

You can join the clothing-optional games that take place on the tennis and volleyball courts, work out in the fitness room, sign up for a clothing-optional cruise to Tintamarre Island on the *Tiko-Tiko* catamaran at the watersports center, or dine alfresco at **Papagayo Restaurant**. But, don't expect to pick up a date or meet your soul mate here. Most guests are with their family or spouse.

★The Mercure Simson Beach
Baie Nettlé
☎ 590-87-54-54, fax 590-87-92-11, www.mercure. com
168 suites and apartments
$$$

Located on the French side of Simpson Bay, just a five-minute drive from Marigot, the Créole-style Mercure is the classiest hotel in its price bracket. Five three-story buildings surround a large swimming pool next to an open-air restaurant that serves a huge complimentary breakfast buffet and a vast patio used for nightly parties featuring island bands.

Each nicely furnished unit has an outdoor kitchenette on the patio or balcony, ceiling fans, and a basic shower-only bathroom. If you want more room, ask for a third-floor suite with high ceilings, a sleeping loft, and an extra bathroom. The landscaped grounds merge with the palm-shaded white-sand beach, which has a dive shop and watersports center. A pay-as-you-go shuttle will drop you in Marigot or Philipsburg for a day of shopping.

★★ Grand Case Beach Club

Grand Case

☎ 888-845-5821, 590-87-51-87, fax 590-87-59-93, www.gcbc.com

73 studios and one- and two-bedroom suites

$$$$

AUTHOR'S PICK
MID-SIZE RESORT
★

Located on a quiet stretch of sand east of Grand Case, this popular hotel caters to return guests who enjoy lounging about all day dreaming of the delicacies they will enjoy for dinner at one of the gourmet restaurants down the road. To that end, the resort provides comfortable accommodations in low-rise buildings clustered on landscaped grounds adjacent to a swimming pool, lighted tennis court, well-run watersports center, dive

shop, and the casual **Sunset Café**. Each unit has all the amenities you'd expect in a three-star resort, but the furnishings are informal rather than luxurious. Many bedrooms have king-size beds, the kitchenettes have a microwave and small refrigerator, every studio and suite has a patio or balcony, and the sandy beach is no more than a hundred feet from your door.

★★★L'Esplanade Caraïbes Hotel

Grand Case

☎ 590-670-0655, fax 590-87-29-15, www.lesplanade. com

4 condos

$$$$

AUTHOR'S
TOP PICK
OVERALL

Views from this resort's hillside perch are truly spectacular. You look out over the sea, the beach, and the row of gourmet restaurants in the quaint village of Grand Case, and ponder the dilemma of what to do next. Walk

down to the white-sand beach? Dress for dinner? Simply continue to sit on your private terrace and stare at the hypnotic turquoise water?

We especially liked the spacious loft units

on the top floor of this pretty stucco-and-wood resort. They cost a bit more than a studio, but they have a sleeper sofa and half-bath in the living area, and a king-size bed in the upstairs master suite, which includes a full bathroom. Lofts, studios, and one-bedroom suites all have balconies and well-equipped kitchens with standard-sized refrigerators. If you don't have the energy to walk down the hill to the beach, the hotel has a large pool surrounded by flowering bougainvillea and an adjacent bar.

★★Le Petit Hotel

Grand Case

☎ 590-29-09-65, fax 590-87-09-19, www.lepetithotel. com

Nine studios and one one-bedroom suite

$$$$

AUTHOR'S PICK
SMALL HOTEL

★

All accommodations at this little hotel are excellent, but ask for one of the beach-front units with a private terrace facing the sea – one of the best features of the resort. Each suite also features a king-size bed, ceiling fans as well as air conditioning, and a well-equipped kitchen. You can use the pool at sister resort Hôtel L'Esplanade Caraïbes (a short distance away), and walk to Restaurant Row in Grand Case. Manager Kristen Petrelluzi is an expert on the nearby gourmet offerings and will gladly advise you. If you want to stay in your room, you can borrow DVDs from the office to watch on your TV. A continental breakfast is included in the room price.

St. Martin

Green Cay Village
Orient Bay

☎ 800-832-2302 (in the US) or 590-87-38-63, fax 590-87-39-27

www.greencay.com

16 villas

$$$

Investigate Green Cay Village if you want the intimacy of a villa and the amenities of a good hotel. The spacious units have one, two, or three bedrooms; a living room with lots of entertainment equipment that opens onto a private deck with a small pool and breathtaking views of the bay; and a full kitchen with a large refrigerator. Each West Indies-style villa is a stand-alone structure set in a landscaped garden so that the pool and deck have total privacy.

Honeymooners will value the extra seclusion of the hilltop cottages. Families and friends traveling together will treasure the private bathrooms adjacent to each bedroom, and the guest bath conveniently located next to the living area. Every detail is carefully planned for your comfort and convenience: most of the bedrooms have king-size beds; the decks have plenty of lounge chairs; the outdoor dining area is covered; the cable TV is equipped with a VCR.

Caribbean Princess Condos & Cap Caraïbes Hotel
Orient Bay

☎ 590-52-07-12, fax 590-52-07-13

www.cap-caraibes.com/condos.htm

12 two- or three-bedroom condos and 35 suites

$$$$ condos; $$$ hotel

This is a fairly new complex – expensive, and worth it. Every Princess condo is huge, up to 2,000 square feet, and has two or three bedrooms with one king-size bed or two double beds, large bathrooms connected  to each sleeping area, a full kitchen, a living area with a sleeper sofa, and a spacious furnished patio with great views. Skylights, teak, natural stone, and plenty of glass give rooms an airy, contemporary touch.

The adjacent three-story **Cap Caraibes Hotel** has large suites with small, fully-equipped kitchens and either one king-size or two full-size beds. Sliding doors open onto a furnished patio or balcony, and the third-floor rooms have a marvelous view of Orient Bay. The entire complex is quiet, uncrowded and protected by security guards. Don't expect a lot of resort facilities, but there is a small pool and Orient Beach is just steps away.

Orient Bay Hotel

Orient Bay

☎ 800-818-5992 (in the US) or 590-87-31-10, fax 590-87-37-66

www.orientbayhotel.com

31 one- and two-bedroom villas

$$$

Don't confuse this hotel with the naturalist resort, Club Orient. Here, everyone wears clothes when they swim in one of the two pools or dine in the restaurant. We can't vouch for the attire in the bungalows, which have full kitchens and two terraces. Larger units can accommodate up to five people in two bedrooms, each with an adjoining bathroom. Clothing is, of course, optional at nearby Orient Beach, a five-minute down-

hill walk. Don't book here if you have mobility restrictions. The villas are perched on a lanscaped hillside. Smaller, less expensive studio units are available at the **Jardins de Chevrise** next door ($$, same contact information).

Captain Oliver's Resort

Oyster Pond

☎ 590-87-40-26, fax 590-87-40-84, www.captainolivers.com

50 units

$$$

Popular with both European and American travelers, this attractive resort straddles the French-Dutch border as it crosses Oyster Pond, and is the only hotel grounds in the world that sit partly on French soil and fronting Dutch waters. Staying here is truly an international experience.

More than a hundred luxury yachts are docked at the full-facility marina, and some rooms overlook the wharf. The better view, however, is from one of the spacious ocean-view bungalows. Each unit is in a dusty-rose-colored hillside building and features bathrooms with double sinks and spacious closets. Larger suites have two beds, a sleeper sofa, and a kitchen.

The compound has all sorts of facilities and services. In addition to the marina, there's a glass-walled swimming pool with a deck that extends out into the lagoon and a full-service restaurant serving French and Créole food. The **Dingy Dock bar** has pool tables and serves light meals. The **Iguana Bar** is built over the lagoon and features a two-for-one happy hour from 5-7 pm each evening. You can arrange a deep-sea fishing trip at the marina or schedule a scuba outing at the on-site dive shop. The resort's taxi boat will shuttle you over to Dawn Beach whenever you like.

Watch where you step. The property is alive with parrots, toucans, turtles, monkeys, iguanas – even an alligator.

St. Tropez des Caraïbes Beach Club

Orient Bay

☎ 590-87-42-01, fax 590-87-41-69, www.st-tropez-caraïbes.com

28 suites

$$

Don't expect a beachfront location or a lot of club-type amenities here. The fancy name may lead you to expect grand things that the hotel just does not deliver. Even so, you'll be on Orient Bay, an easy stroll away from the famous French-side beach, at a very reasonable price.

The most spacious accommodations are at the top of each of the four three-level peach-and-sand-colored buildings, which are linked by sidewalks that meander through lush tropical vegetation. Each of the units is clean and nicely furnished with king-size beds and cable TV. A few of the suites have a small kitchenette, and every unit has a microwave and tiny refrigerator.

Hotel Beach Plaza

Marigot Bay

☎ 590-87-87-00, fax 590-87-18-87, www.hotelbeachplazasxm.com

144 rooms and suites

$$$

We were infatuated with this hotel the moment we stepped into its garden-like atrium lobby, and true love followed as we discovered its other appealing attributes. The location couldn't be better: on the French side, between the ocean and Simpson Bay La-

goon, within walking distance of the restaurants and shops in Marigot.

All of the rooms have balconies (ask for a room on the ocean side), appealing decor, cable TV, a small refrigerator, and either one king-size or two twin-size beds.

The hotel beach isn't terrific (small and rocky), but watersports are available, lounge chairs and umbrellas are scattered around the short length of sand and there's a deck built out over the water. **Le Corsaire** restaurant starts the morning with a big American-style buffet breakfast, then switches to French cuisine at lunch and dinner. While the food is good and some dishes spectacular, the views are stunning. Every table at this open-air pool-side restaurant has a marvelous view of the bay, and you'll be tempted to enjoy all your meals there.

Where to Eat

We probably don't need to tell you that the best restaurants are on the French side. While it's possible to eat quite well on Dutch soil, the most ex-

DINING PRICE CHART	
$	under $20
$$	$21-$30
$$$	$31-$40
$$$$	over $40

quisite gourmet meals are prepared in Grand Case, the epicurean capital of St. Martin. Even the waterside open-air *lo-los* serve up tasty island favorites and tender meats grilled on oil-drum barbecue pits. In Marigot, you'll enjoy dining alfresco at one of the bistros facing Marina la Port Royale; at the beach-side restaurants on Orient Bay, your delicious eclectic cuisine will most likely be accompanied by live music.

On the Dutch side, look for delicious international dishes – Indonesian, Indian, and Italian. Philipsburg has a few outstanding eateries, but more variety is found along Airport Road, and Welfare Road on the Simpson Bay lagoon. Fresh seafood, both locally caught and imported, is the mainstay of these restaurants, but many also serve steaks brought in from the US.

Since food service is a flaky business dependent on the chefs' moods, economic situations, and constantly-changing trends, most of our suggestions are for restaurants that have a longstanding reputation. New places open regularly, so eavesdrop on conversations and ask around to find out where people have recently had a great meal.

Island Dining

- Make dinner **reservations**, especially during high season.

- **Call ahead** to verify seasonal time changes and closings.

- Shorts and jeans are OK **attire** for most places, but dress up a bit for the finest restaurants: slacks and sport shirts for men; sundresses or slacks for women.

- Unless noted otherwise, restaurant **hours** are noon until 3 pm for lunch and 6 until 10:30 pm for dinner. If breakfast is served, the restaurant typically opens at 7:30 am. French-side restaurants usually close completely between lunch and dinner, while most Dutch-side restaurants stay open throughout the afternoon, though they may serve only a limited menu. If you plan to eat outside these normal hours of operation, call the restaurant to be sure it's open.

- Nearly all restaurants accept major **credit cards**, with the exception of a few small cafés, beach vendors, and fast-food establishments.

■ Pick up free copies of **Ti Gourmet** and **St. Martin Nights** at your hotel or one of the tourist offices. These guides are filled with good restaurant information, including hours of operation and phone numbers, but feature only businesses that pay to be included.

Use the following scale as a guide to what a typical dinner will cost each person, excluding drinks and service charge or tip. Breakfast and lunch prices will be lower.

No tax is charged on meals, but Dutch-side restaurants often add a 15% service charge, which may or may not go to the waitstaff, so it's customary to leave a bit more for good service. If no service fee is added, leave the usual 10-20% tip. French-side restaurants include the service charge in the price of the meal, but it's customary to leave an additional 5-10% more on the table as appreciation for good service since the service charge is usually shared among all employees in the restaurant.

Restaurant Directory

GRAND CASE
Lo-Lo Fast Food, no phone
Sunset Café, Grand Case Beach Resort, north of town, ☎ 590-87-51-87, fax 590-87-17-74
Auberge Gourmande, 89 Boulevard de Grand Case, ☎ 590-87-73-37, fax 590-29-24-46
Bistrot Caraïbes, 81 Boulevard de Grand Case, ☎ 590-29-08-29, fax 590-29-08-29
Le Tastevin, 86 Boulevard de Grand Case, ☎ 590-87-55-45, fax 590-87-55-45
Le Cottage, 97 Boulevard de Grand Case, ☎ 590-29-03-30
Il Nettuno, 70 Boulevard de Grand Case, ☎ 590-87-77-38, fax 590-87-77-38
Le Pressoir, 30 Boulevard de Grand Case, ☎ 590-87-76-62

In Grand Case

Lo-Lo Fast Food

If you're on a tight budget, or just want to have a tasty meal while hangin' with the locals, stop at one of the half-dozen *lo-los* set up along the main drag south of the fishing pier. These outdoor eateries run by local cooks are such an important part of the town's culinary scene that the government financed their rebirth after Hurricane Luis wrecked them several years ago.

You don't need a map to find them. Just follow your nose and the smoke wafting skyward from the makeshift barbecue pits. Menus are handwritten on blackboards, but don't bother reading the selections. Everything is laid out before you on a blazing oil-drum grill.

Ribs are popular, and the half-chickens are always tempting, but we suggest grilled fish or lobster. You won't find it fresher or cheaper anywhere else on the island. Patrons walk away carrying Styrofoam plates piled high with mixed grill and side-dishes for well under $10.

> **Tip:** *During high season (Jan-April), Grand Case sponsors **Harmony Nights** on Tuesday night at 6 pm. The roads are closed to cars (park on the soccer field) and strollers enjoy music, art exhibits and restaurant specials.*

Sunset Café

Grand Case Beach Club Resort, north of town

☎ 590-87-51-87, www.sunset-cafe.com

American, French $$

Open all day for breakfast, lunch, and dinner

Buzz at the front gate and announce your intention to dine in order to gain entry to the resort grounds. During the day, this is a fine way to gain access to the resort's stretch of fine sand that separates Grand Case Beach from Petite Plage and overlooks Creole Rock. Order a croissant or full American breakfast, then set-

St. Martin

BEST SUNSET VIEW

tle yourself on the beach. The lounge chairs have flags that you raise whenever you want something from the bar. At lunchtime, order a burger or salad, stay on for happy hour drinks, then linger over a candlelight French dinner prepared by chef Jean-Pierre.

(Don't confuse this with Sunset Beach Bar near the Dutch-side airport on Maho Beach.)

L'Auberge Gourmande

89 Boulevard de Grand Case

☎ 590-87-73-37, www.laubergegourmande.com

French $$$

Dinner only

Set in a lovely refurbished old Creole house, the romantic surroundings alone are worth the price of dinner, especially if you sit at one of the tables on the tiny porch. The waitresses wear halter tops and shorts, so the atmosphere is casual and unassuming. Take your time and enjoy each beautiful presentation as it comes to your table from chef Didier Rochat's kitchen. An apricot champagne cocktail.  Warm foie gras. Pumpkin and crab bisque. A bit of smoked salmon. Perfectly grilled inch-thick tuna steak with a pink center and a sun-dried tomato crust, accompanied by pesto mashed potatoes. Or, perhaps the veal sweetbreads. You won't find them prepared as well, or at all, back home. Finish with a rich dessert. The friendly staff will help you choose the perfect wine from their well-stocked cellar, without a hint of intimidation.

St. Martin

Bistrot Caraïbes

81 Boulevard de Grand Case

☎ 590-29-08-29, www.bistrotcaraibes.com

French/Creole $$$

Dinner only

You walk past the live lobster pool when you enter this cozy bistro on your way to a candlelit table. Thibault and Amaury, brother chefs from Lyon, France, personally oversee the kitchen and dining room, so you are guaranteed a wonderful meal. If you don't order lobster, consider the scallops drizzled with garlic butter, grilled rack of lamb, or one of the nightly specials. The highlight for dessert is homemade ice cream.

★ Le Tastevin

86 Boulevard de Grand Case

☎ 590-87-55-45

French $$$

BEST LUNCH

★ Reserve a table overlooking the beach. The view will add to your dining experience, especially at lunch, when there's plenty of activity to watch. At lunch, order one of the creative salads or rich soups. In the evening, ask about the chef's specials – you can't go wrong with roasted duck or grilled fish. Almost every entrée is dressed with a colorful, tangy sauce and matched with perfectly grilled vegetables. The restaurant's name hints at a well-stocked wine cellar, so ask the staff for suggestions.

Le Cottage

97 Boulevard de Grand Case

☎ 590-29-03-30, www.restaurantlecottage.com

French $$$

Dinner only

There's no view of the sea from this lovely white stucco restaurant, but you won't miss it. The yellow and blue plates and dining room décor will remind you of sunny Provence; the colorfully tiled lobster tank is strikingly Caribbean. Creative dishes from the kitchen include pumpkin soup, foie gras with unusual sauces (even chocolate), duck confit, almond-crusted beef tenderloin, and homemade sorbet. Ask the sommelier to help you select a different glass of wine to go with each course of your dinner. The restaurant claims to have the most extensive wine list on the island, and offers the most wines by the glass, so take this opportunity to try several different vintages. Look for owner Bruno Lemoine, who learned his profession in the restaurants of Paris, as he roams among the tables visiting with customers.

Il Nettuno

70 Boulevard de Grand Case

☎ 590-87-77-38, www.ilnettuno.com

Italian $$$

The owner, Ramon, is from the US, and the chefs are from various parts of Europe, but the cuisine is mouth-watering Italian. Hunger-spiking aromas coming from the kitchen indicate a liberal use of garlic and spices, and may cause you to be impatient, but take your time mulling over the large menu as you nibble the bruschetta delivered to your table by the friendly staff. On a recent visit with Italian-American friends, the tender fried calamari appetizer was a big hit. Next time, we plan to try the house specialty, sautéed shrimp in white wine and garlic. The much-acclaimed Saltimbocca alla Romana (veal scallops and prosciuto ham rolled around fresh herbs) lived up to its superb reputation, and the vegetarian in our group raved about the homemade pasta. Terrific Italian wines are available by the glass.

★Le Pressoir

30 Boulevard de Grand Case

☎ 590-87-76-62

French $$$

Dinner only

Located in one of the oldest houses on the island, this charming country-French restaurant is on many visitors' must-do list because of the flawless service and superb cuisine. Stephane Mabille, the owner-chef, is quite proud of his well-stocked wine cellar and will

suggest a great vintage to accompany your meal. On a recent visit, our group sampled traditional scallops St-Jacques (sweet and tender), roasted duck in ginger sauce (moist without being oily), and a vegetable tart. We thought we had been transported to France – or heaven. Things only improved when we savored warm chocolate cake topped with vanilla ice cream for dessert.

Restaurant Directory

MARIGOT
Don Carmello, Marina Royale ☎ 590-87-52-88
La Belle Epoque, Marina Royale, ☎ 590-87-87-70
La Main à la Pâte, Marina Royale, ☎ 590-87-71-19
Le Chanteclair, Marina Royale, ☎ 590-87-94-60
La Petite Auberge des Îles, Marina Royale, ☎ 590-87-56-31
Le Saint Germain, ☎ 590-87-92-87
Le Bar de la Mer, Waterfront, ☎ 590-29-03-82
La Vie en Rose, Boulevard de France, ☎ 590-87-54-42

In Marigot

Marina Royale

It's a lot of fun to eat at one of the open-air restaurants lining the boardwalk of Marina Royale in Marigot. The atmosphere is casual, and the food is wonderful. If you're a true gourmet, you will want to stick to the two dozen restaurants lining the main boulevard in Grand Case, but the average palate won't be able to discern a great difference between the fare offered in these two towns.

As in France, all the restaurants post their menus and nightly specials outside the dining room, so you can spend a leisurely half-hour strolling along the waterfront comparing dishes and prices. Many of the postings will seem to be similar, which may make your decision difficult. We always choose the eatery with the biggest crowd. Below are a few of our favorites, followed by the name and phone number of others along the boardwalk.

   During high season, the Marigot Waterfront sponsors a mini-festival on Wednesday and Sunday nights, featuring live bands, clowns, and dance lessons. Make your restaurant reservation well in advance.

★La Petite Auberge des Îles
☎ 590-87-56-31

French and Créole $$

Monday-Saturday, 11:30 am-11 pm

This is one of the smallest cafés around the marina, and tables spill out of the tiny dining area onto the boardwalk. Just wiggle into any smidgen of space that's available and prepare for a fantastic treat. Owners Françoise and Bruno Darricarrere will make you feel like old friends almost immediately, with Bruno hustling around tending bar and waiting tables, while Françoise periodically dashes out of the kitchen to chat. You won't go wrong ordering the nightly special, but start with the escargot drenched in garlic butter and finish with profiteroles.

La Belle Epoque
☎ 590-87-87-70, www.belle-epoque-sxm.com

French $$

Monday-Saturday, 7:30 am-11 pm

When this bistro is crowded, the service suffers a bit, but your meal will be excellent when it arrives. Everything from pizza to steak is popular, but we especially like the French onion soup and the salmon with basil sauce. Diners nearby said the lobster was delicious, and friends from Chicago (where everyone is a pizza expert) voted the Roquefort-chèvre-mozzarella pizza the best they'd ever tasted.

★Le Main à la Pâte

☎ 590-87-71-19

French $$

Monday-Saturday, 11:30 am-11 pm

The name translates *hand in the dough*, but loosely means the chef makes everything from scratch. We sampled several things and found the Caribbean Sea-food Pot (pasta, clams, shrimp, and mahi-mahi in tomato sauce) and the red snapper in passion sauce outstanding. Our French waiter was friendly and gave good advice about ordering from the extensive menu. Prices are very reasonable.

Le Chanteclair

☎ 590-87-94-60

French $$$

Daily, 6-10:30 pm

Chef Cécile's *No Name* dessert (a deep-fried pastry filled with chocolate) is famous, the foie gras is a superb specialty and the grilled tuna is wonderful. The prices are on the high side, but well worth it, since Cécile on the award-winning St. Maarten culinary team. Ask about his recent winning Camilo dishes.

★Don Camillo

☎ 590-87-52-88

Italian $$

Monday-Saturday, 6:30-10:30 pm

Letters and post cards written by dozens of happy, well-fed patrons cover one wall and part of several windows. It takes a truly extraordinary meal to inspire such poetic praise. Enzo, the gracious Sicilian owner and host, sees to your every need and will make suggestions if you find the menu overwhelming. The tomato and mozzarella salad is large enough to share,

St. Martin

portions of homemade pasta are generous, and the homemade bread topped with an anchovy-enhanced spread is addictive. Try the fruit tart for dessert.

Restaurants Elsewhere in Marigot

★ Le Bar de la Mer

Waterfront – near the public market

☎ 590-29-03-82

Varied menu $$

Daily, 8 am-1 am

Everyone eventually comes to Le Bar, and it may seem that they all arrive just when you want to eat. Nudge your way through the crowd around the downstairs bar and make your way up to the dining room on the second floor. At lunch, you can't go wrong with the pizza. Its tantalizing aroma will seduce you as soon as you arrive. For dinner, go for the highly-acclaimed Caribbean barbecue served on the spacious terrace. All kinds of fish and meats are basted with a spicy marinade and grilled to perfection. Fantastic flavors.

★★ La Vie en Rose

Boulevard de France

☎ 590-87-54-42, www.lavieenrosestmartin.com

French $$$$

Daily, 11:30 am-2:30 pm and 6:30-10 pm

AUTHOR'S CHOICE

This is one of the oldest and most popular restaurants on St. Martin. Prices are high, but you should try it. Year after year, it ranks among the best restaurants on the island. It's located in a colonial-style house with a patio that opens out to the street and a second-floor balcony, which is great for people watching. When we arrived during the busy lunchtime, we thought the servers had a bit of a snooty attitude, but on a return visit, this time for dinner, the service was relaxed and gracious. Stick to reasonably priced salads and sandwiches at lunch, but splurge on dinner. Each elegant course will be served slowly to allow you time to enjoy and digest. Choices are fairly typical – roasted duck, rack of lamb, fresh fish – but the sauces and other embellishments are out of this world. Think puff pastry surrounding some type of meat and drizzled with herb-spiked butter, warm raspberry sauce poured over a poultry breast, goat cheese sprinkled over lightly grilled filets. Your surroundings will be as re-markable as the meal – coffered ceilings and candlelight.

Restaurant Directory

St. Martin

PHILIPSBURG
Antoine, Front Street, ☎ 599-542-2964
Greenhouse, Bobby's Marina, ☎ 599-542-2941, www.thegreenhouserestaurant.com
Taloula Mango's, Hendrickstraat, ☎ 599-542-4278

SIMPSON BAY
Cappuccino, Welfare Road, ☎ 599-544-3331
Lee's Road Side Grill, Airport Road, ☎ 599-544-4233, www.leesfish.com
Ric's Place, Airport Road, ☎ 599-545-3630
Ristorante Laguna, Airport Road, ☎ 599-545-2025
Saratoga, Simpson Bay Yacht Club, Airport Road, ☎ 599-544-2421
Skipjack, Airport Road, ☎ 599-544-2313, www.skipjacks-sxm.com
Turtle Pier, Simpson Bay Lagoon Marina/Airport Road, ☎ 599-545-2562

In Philipsburg

Taloula Mango's Caribbean Café

Boardwalk at Great Bay

☎ 599- 542-4278, www.taloulamangos.com

Eclectic $

Daily, 7:30 am-10:30 pm

Like a lot of tourists, we dropped into this trendy wa-terfront restaurant to get a snack and a cold drink, but we came back later for a full meal because we were so impressed by the menu. Specifically, we were tempted by the Rich Mans Fish and Chips, which turned out to be salmon and thick-cut fries. On another visit, we ordered pear-and-parmigiana salads to go with a tuna pizza. Who would have guessed these things would taste so terrific? Turns out the chef is Dino Jagtiani, a graduate of the Culinary Institute. He helped the owners (restaurant veterans Su and Norm Wathey) tweak the menu to add a bit of jazz, and the results are fantastic. The kitchen still turns out a good burger and other traditional fare. The kids can even get a grilled cheese sandwich. A long list of drinks rounds out the offerings, and the view of the bay is unsurpassed.

Antoine

Front Street

☎ 599-542-2964

Italian, Créole, French $$$

Daily, 11:30 am-10 pm

Reservations highly recommended in season

Owners Jean-Pierre Pomarico and Pierre-Louis Kesner oversee this wonderful restaurant, with splendid views of Great Bay. Skip over the Italian dishes, you can find better elsewhere, but the French and Créole meals are as good as any you'll find on the island. Start with freshly made pâté or one of the soups, then ask for guidance on the entrée. Seafood, veal, and beef are on the menu, and Pierre-Louis often prepares a daily special. You can't go wrong with the veal scallopini or steak au poivre, and a *New York Times*' food critic says the lobster thermidor is outstanding.

Greenhouse

Bobby's Marina, Philipsburg

☎ 599-542-2941, www.thegreenhouserestaurant.com

Steak, ribs, lobster $$

Daily, 11 am-midnight, after-hours on Tuesday nights

Happy Hour daily 4:30 pm-7 pm

We were surprised, in a good way, on our recent visits to this open-air restaurant on the capital's harbor.

First, the parking was easy, due to a big new lot at the adjacent marina. Second, the food was as good as rumored. The beef-eaters among us claimed that their steak was better than any they'd had back in the States (the meat, in fact, was black Angus imported from the US), but most of us opted for chicken and fish. Both were delicious, but the mango-salsa chicken breast won out over the snapper in our show-of-hands taste test, even though the fish was obviously fresh and perfectly blackened. After dinner, we played a little pool, and the regulars encouraged us to return on a Tuesday night, when a DJ plays music and oversees a cut-throat trivia contest

St. Martin

In Simpson Bay

★ Ric's Place

Airport Road, lagoon side , near the draw bridge

☎ 599-545-3630, www.ricsplace-sxm.com

Tex-Mex and American $

Daily, 8 am-10 pm

Sports fans flock to this casual, friendly spot to enjoy nachos and beer while they watch back-home events on a big screen. But many locals and tourists who don't know or care about sports ignore the cheering fans, escape to the patio overlooking the lagoon and concentrate on the delicious food. Known for serving a terrific American-style breakfast from  eight until noon, the restaurant also gets raves for its big juicy burgers and crispy fries. If you're in need of a Mexican food fix, you can't do better than the puffy, overstuffed chimichanga or beef enchiladas with all the trimmings.

★★Turtle Pier

Simpson Bay Lagoon Marina/Airport Road

☎ 599-545-2562, www.turtlepier.com

Eclectic and seafood $$

Breakfast, lunch, and dinner daily

We've heard good things about the lobster specials on Wednesday nights, but we don't have first-hand experience. On another night, we were delighted with the coconut shrimp. Jumbo shrimp were coated in beer batter, dipped in coconut and fried to a crispy golden brown. Yummy. Later, we returned for a sandwich lunch, mostly so that we could enjoy a waterside table and look out at the lagoon. Things were a little slow coming out of the kitchen, but we didn't mind since it gave us a chance to wander out to the entrance path to visit with the caged monkeys and parrots. Happy hour runs from 5 to 7 pm every day, and this is the perfect spot to watch the sunset over the lagoon. Live music plays several nights each week during high season, and kids of all ages will enjoy watching turtles, parrots, monkeys and rabbits frolicking in their pens.

Saratoga

Simpson Bay Yacht Club, Airport Road

☎ 599-544-2421

Seafood $$

Daily, 6:30-10:30 pm; closed Aug and Sept

Call ahead for a table near the water – you'll enjoy your meal even more. The menu changes frequently, and always features fresh seafood. Chef John Jackson (from Saratoga Springs, New York) cooks with an Asian flair, which tends to be lower in fat. If you've had your fill of seafood, look for steaks, chicken, duck, and pork dishes. Everything is well prepared, so you can't make a bad choice.

Peg Leg

Three Palms Plaza, Simpson Bay

☎ 599-544-5859, www.peglegpub.com

Steak, pasta, home cooking $

Monday-Saturday, 11 am-11 pm, Sunday 4-11 pm

Happy Hour daily 4-6 pm

You remember ol' Peg Leg, don't you? Peter Stuyvesant, from Holland, who became governor of the island of Curaçao, lost a leg fighting the Portuguese for control of Sint Maarten, and finally became governor of New York, where he staunchly pushed for better taverns. Ol' Peg Leg would be very proud of this pub that carries his nickname

He would no doubt prop his wooden leg up on a stool at the stretch and settle in to sample some of the more than 30 types of bottled and tap beer. If it was an election year, he'd offer to buy a round of specialty drinks for his pals, then dig into the chef's Blue Plate Special (served daily during lunch hour). While the pub is known among locals as a great steakhouse, the menu offers something for everyone. Ol' Pete was a carnivore, but even he would appreciate the excellent pasta dishes.

Pizza Galley

Airport Road, Simpson Bay

☎ 599-557-7416, www.pizzagalley.com.

$

Monday-Saturday 6-11 pm

When you ask a local where to find the island's best pizza, they'll direct you to the Galley. Owners JP and Lorna take pizza seriously and make their pies fresh daily from top-quality ingredients and better-than-average imagination. A basic cheese pie (ask for Bare Naked) is a bargain at $9, and you can get really fancy with the Surf and Turf (steak, shrimp, veggies and goat cheese) for about $18. Add a glass of wine and one of Lorna's prize-winning desserts for a truly great meal. Look for the sign on the dock near the draw bridge beside the Lady C Floating Bar, and call ahead for take-out.

Lee's Road Side Grill

Airport Road, Simpson Bay

☎ 599-544-4233, www.leesfish.com

Seafood $$

Daily 10 am-midnight

Happy hour daily 4-7 pm

Leonel Halley's passion is fish and fishing. He owns Lee's Deep-Sea Fishing, a charter operation, as well as the popular Lee's Road Side Grill and Bar. (When you think about it, you have to wonder why all fishermen don't own a seafood restaurant.) He's a tournament-winning fisherman with a love of the sea, and his enthusiasm spills over into his restaurant business. His fishing boats come in around five every afternoon, and the catch heads straight to the roadside kitchen. You just can't get seafood any fresher than this. If you're one of the rare folks who don't care for fresh fish, the menu has a variety of other options, all served with salad and a potato dish. The drinks are good too, and it's difficult to decide whether to come in early for happy hour or stay late to enjoy the live band that starts up about eight o'clock most evenings. No reason, really, why you can't do both.

Ristorante Laguna

Airport Road, Simpson Bay

☎ 599-545-2025

Italian $$

Daily, 6-10:30 pm

Call to reserve a table on the outside terrace so you can watch the light change over the lagoon as the sun sets. Then enjoy your exquisite meal by starlight.

Owners Franco Patanée and Gianni Tirocchi started out in the restaurant business in their native Italy and have run three restaurants on St. Martin during the past 25 years. It goes without saying, they know their stuff. All pasta dishes are cooked to perfection, but those with seafood are particularly delicious. On a recent visit, we tried the linguine tossed with olive oil, garlic, lobster and shrimp. It was sheer Tuscan bliss. Equally delicious, the broiled lamb chop. We could go on about the desserts and espresso, but some pleasures are best experienced for oneself.

Skipjack

Airport Road, Simpson Bay

☎ 599-544-2313, www.skipjacks-sxm.com.

Fish $$

Daily, 11 am-11 pm

This is a relatively new restaurant, but the restauranteur has been a popular fixture on the island for a long time. Brad Belding is the former proprietor of Hot Tomatoes and Sunset Beach Bar. Now, he's become a fishmonger. The glass case in front of Skipjack displays fresh-as-they-come Maine and Caribbean lobsters, crab, a variety of fish and sashimi-grade tuna. All for sale to take home. For those who prefer to let the chef do the work, the main dining room is decorated in a nautical theme, and the outside deck overlooks the lagoon. Even people who don't eat fish like Skipjack's because the menu also features some steak, and chicken selections. Everything is served with rice or potatoes and some type of grilled veggies

Cappuccino

Welfare Road, Simpson Bay

☎ 599-544-3331

Diner/Coffee House/Bar $

24-hour service daily

You can find more gourmet meals at a hundred different restaurants scattered around the island, but this unpretentious, open-air bar and grill manages the basics very well. Order breakfast at any time of day. Get

St. Martin

a burger or pizza whenever you want it. Find an amiable bartender after all the other bars have closed for the night. You can even get a decent steak here at a very reasonable price. Two big-screen TVs show sporting events or back-home news, the service is fast and friendly, and you'll get plenty to eat.

Nightlife

St. Martin is not an island that goes dark after the sun sets. Dutch-side casinos, bars, and clubs go strong until the early morning hours, and frequently changing hot spots draw a sleek party crowd. You'll have to ask around to find out where the best bands are playing and the best drinks are being poured while you're on the island, but we've listed a few of the always-popular places. Also, check the entertainment listings in free publications such as *St. Maarten Nights.* You'll find copies in hotel lobbies, restaurants, and at the tourist office.

If there's a full moon, you must go to **Kali's Beach Bar** on Friar's Bay, ☎ 590-51-07-44. There will be a big bonfire on the beach and dancing to a live reggae band until the sun comes up. During high season (January-April) Grand Case throws a street party called **Harmony Nights** beginning just before sunset on Tuesday evenings. Marigot hosts a similar event on Wednesday and Sunday nights. Both mini-festivals feature live bands, artist booths, clowns and other entertainment.

Pineapple Pete, at Royal Village on Welfare Road (☎ 599-544-6030), closes the restaurant at around 10:30 every night, but the bar and pool room stay open until the early morning hours. Regulars show up most nights to play a bit of pool and tip a pint or two, and the word is spreading about the live entertainment on Tuesday, Friday and Saturday nights. If you want to have dinner, make a reservation, because this is a popular spot with the boating crowd who arrive by dinghy.

Several evenings per week, depending on the season, you can join the **Pub Crawl** aboard the 40-foot catamaran *Celine*. Leaving Turtle Pier around 7 pm, the boat cruises around Simpson Bay Lagoon, stopping for a half-hour or so at various pubs along the way. At each stop, you get a drink and some type of appetizer, then move on. Celine also has an open bar, so the party gains strength quickly. The cost is approximately $65 per person, and you'll return to your starting point on the pier at about 10:30 pm. ☎ 599-545-3961.

 From May through November, the island is quieter and many residents leave for their own vacation. Call ahead or check with the tourist office to verify that specific activities will be taking place before you make plans.

Popular Clubs & Bars

★**The Green House**, Bobby's Marina, Philipsburg, ☎ 599-542-2941.Now the best place for live music, dancing, and happy hour on Tuesday nights.

Sopranos Piano Bar, Maho Plaza, ☎ 599-545-2485, www.sopranospianobar.com. No cover charge; live music nightly.

The Hideaway, La Vista Resort, ☎ 599-544-3005, ext. 1132. Thursday and Saturday nights, this restaurant hosts a one-man band. You can join in with karaoke.

Captain Oliver's, Oyster Pond, ☎ 590-87-40-26. Call for a reservation for the Saturday night lobster buffet and dance party with live music.

Friar's Beach Club, Friar's Bay, ☎ 590-49-16-87. Drop by on Sunday nights for dancing to music provided by a local band.

Bliss, Caravanserai Resort, Simpson Bay, ☎ 599-545-3996, www.theblissexperience.com. An open-air club with techno music and a swimming pool.

Sunset Beach Bar, at the end of the runway on Airport Beach, ☎ 599-545-3998, www.sunsetbeachbar. com. A gazebo on the sand that is popular with locals and tourists who like to watch the planes land as they enjoy $1 shooters, tropical drinks and live music. This is the place to watch for the elusive "greenflash" in the sky the minute the sun sets.

Kon Tiki, Orient Beach, ☎ 590-29-01-85, is a shack on the beach that is popular with a young single crowd. Live music most nights.

Casinos

On any night of the week, you can try your luck at the casinos on the Dutch side. The dealers are friendly and laid back, so you won't have the pressure common at serious Las Vegas game tables.

Slots take US currency, and entertainment is scheduled most nights of the week.

Atlantis, Cupecoy, ☎ 599-545-4601, www. atlantiscasino.com

★**Casino Royale**, Maho Reef, ☎ 599-545-2590. More than 200 slots and 16 blackjack tables. The adjacent **Showroom Royale** features Vegas-style shows.

Coliseum, Front Street, Philipsburg, ☎ 599-543-2101

Diamond Casino, Front Street, Philipsburg, ☎ 599-543-2583

★**Dolphin Casino**, Caravanserai Beach Resort, ☎ 599-545-3707

Golden Casino, Little Bay, ☎ 599-542-2446

Hollywood Casino, Simpson Bay, ☎ 599-544-4463

★**Princess Casino**, Cole Bay, ☎ 599-544-5222

Rouge and Noir Casino, Front Street, Philipsburg, ☎ 599-542-2952. This is a favorite with cruise-ship visitors.

Tropicana Casino, Cole Bay, ☎ 599-544-5654

Island Facts & Numbers

AIRPORTS: Princess Juliana on the Dutch side, ☎ 599-545-4211, www.pjiae.com. The airport code is SMX. (Juliana became Queen of the Netherlands after the airport was built.) Most international flights arrive at this larger airport. **L'Espérance** is on the French side, ☎ 590-87-53-03. The airport code is SFG. This airport accepts only small aircraft.

AREA CODES: 590 on the French side; 599 on the Dutch side. (See *Telephone* below.)

ATMS & BANKS: Cash machines are scattered in convenient locations throughout both the French and Dutch sides of St. Martin.

 ATMs on the Dutch side dispense US dollars; those on the French side dispense euros. Some machines give you a choice.

BUSES: Private mini-buses and vans travel the main roads between Philipsburg, Marigot, Grand Case, and the large residential areas. Fares are inexpensive, around $1 or $2, depending on the distance, but you may have to change vehicles several times to reach your destination. Buses/vans, which are meant for local workers, are crowded during morning and afternoon rush hours. Few or no vehicles provide service at night.

CAPITALS: Philipsburg (Dutch) and **Marigot** (French).

CELL PHONES: Eastern Caribbean Cellular (☎ 599-542-2100, fax 599-542-5678, www.eastcaribbeancellular.com) and **Cellular One** (☎ 599-545-2430 in Simpson Bay and ☎ 599-543-0222 in Philipsburg) will program your personal cell phone for use on the island at a reasonable price. Consider bringing and activating two phones if you want to keep in touch with friends or family who are also on the island. (If you don't own a cell phone, you can rent one while on the island.)

You may be able to have your home phone programmed with an international calling plan which allows people at home to call you on the island for less than 50¢ a minute – a great savings and particularly convenient if you need to stay in touch with kids or elderly relatives. Not all telephone services offer this option, and AT&T charges their customers a small monthly fee for the international calling plan.

CREDIT CARDS: Most large restaurants, hotels, businesses, and shops accept major credit cards. Ask before you shop, if the credit card symbols are not displayed in the window. Small establishments deal mainly in cash, especially on the French side.

DEPARTURE TAX: $30 for all visitors over the age of two.

DRINKING WATER: Most people drink bottled water, and it is sold everywhere throughout the island. However, water served in restaurants and used in hotel bathrooms is collected rain water or desalinated sea water. It's safe to drink, but you may not care for the taste. Children, elderly people, and anyone with a sensitive stomach or immune problem should stick to bottled water.

DRESS: Wear swimsuits and other skimpy clothing only on the beaches and around the pools. Otherwise, shorts and other casual wear are appropriate during the day. People dress up a bit for restaurant dinners, casinos, and nightclubs, but there's no need for a jacket or tie, unless you go someplace really elegant. You may need a light sweater in the evening, especially if the wind is blowing.

ELECTRICITY: 220 volts on the French side and plugs must fit French outlets. Appliances made for use in North America require a converter and a plug adapter. Those made for European use may run hot. It's 110 volts on the Dutch side and appliances made for use in North America do not need a converter or plug adapter. Those made for European use require a converter and adapter.

EMERGENCY NUMBERS:

Dutch

Fire, **Police**, **Medical Emergency**, ☎ 911.

Non-emergency calls: Fire, ☎ 542-6001; **Police**, ☎ 542-2111/542-2112; **Police patrol** or **sea rescue**, ☎ 542-2222; **Ambulance**, ☎ 542-2111; **Hospital**, ☎ 543-1111.

French

Fire, **Police**, **Medical Emergency**, ☎ 18.

Non-emergency calls: **Police**, ☎ 590-87-73-84; **Fire**, ☎ 590-87-50-08; **Ambulance**, ☎ 590-87-86-25 (daytime) or 590-87-72-00 (at night); **Hospital**, ☎ 590-29-57-57.

HIGHEST POINT: Paradise Peak (Pic Paradis) at 1,391 feet.

INTERNET: Many of the large resorts have Internet access for their guests, but if your hotel doesn't, try the **Cyber Café** at the Yacht Club on Simpson Bay or **Dockside Management** at Bobby's Marina in Philipsburg. Wireless service is becoming more available island-wide.

LAND AREA: 36 square miles total. French side = 20 square miles; Dutch side = 16 square miles.

LANGUAGE: Most residents on the Dutch side and many on the French side speak English. Many residents also speak a French-based patois, and perhaps some Spanish.

However, the official language of Dutch St. Martin is Dutch, and some people speak Papiamento, the language spoken on Aruba and other Dutch Caribbean islands. The official language of French St. Martin is French, and a large number of residents speak little or nothing else.

MONEY: On the Dutch side, the official currency is the **Netherlands Antilles florin** (1.75 NAF = $1), but US dollars are accepted almost everywhere. If prices are quoted in florins, the quick math is to divide the total by two then add 10%.

St. Martin

On the French side, the official currency is the **euro** which is within a few pennies of equaling $1. US dollars are widely accepted, but not as welcome as on the Dutch side. If you pay in dollars, expect change back in euros.

NEWSPAPERS: The English-language *The Daily Herald,* ☎ 599-542-5253; in French, *Saint Martin's Week,* ☎ 590-87-78-67.

PHARMACIES: **Central Drugstore**, ☎ 599-542-2321 (in Philipsburg); **The Druggist**, ☎ 599-545-2777 (in Simpson Bay); **Caraïbes**, ☎ 590-87-47-27 (in Cul-de-Sac); **Grand Case**, ☎ 590-87-77-46 (in Grand Case).

POLITICAL STATUS: Dutch St. Martin is politically tied to the Kingdom of the Netherlands and is part of the six-island group known as The Netherlands ntilles. The island of Curaçao serves as the seat of government. French St. Martin is politically tied to the island of Guadeloupe, which is an Overseas Region of France. (For more details, see page 40.)

POPULATION: Approximately 69,000.

POST OFFICE: The main post office is on Cannegieter Street, near the intersection with Schoolsteeg, in Philipsburg, ☎ 599-542-2298.

RADIO STATIONS: **Radio Transat**, 106.1 FM, ☎ 590-87-55-55. **PJD-1 Mix FM**, 94.7 FM, ☎ 599-543-1133.

TAXIS: Taxis are plentiful at the airport and ferry docks. Drivers are licensed by either the French or Dutch government and carry a published rate sheet, which lists authorized fares between many common destinations, such as from the airport to major hotels. Ask to see it. Daytime rates apply from 7 am to 9 pm. An additional 25% is added to the base fare from 9 until midnight; 50% is added from midnight to 7 am. If your destination isn't listed, negotiate a price before you get into the cab, and confirm whether the rate quoted is per-trip or per-passenger.

Unless the driver overcharges, is rude, or takes you out of your way, add at least a 10% tip to the fare. Tip a little extra if the driver gives information about the island as you travel or helps you with your luggage ($1 per bag is standard, depending on the size and weight of each piece). US dollars and euros are accepted, but don't expect the driver to have change for large-denomination bills.

Taxi Dispatch Hotline, ☎ 147. You can also call the individual taxi stands: in **Philipsburg**, Dutch St. Martin, ☎ 599-542-2359; at the **airport** on Dutch St. Martin, ☎ 599-5435-4317; in **Marigot**, French St. Martin, ☎ 0590-87-56-54; at the airport in **Grand Case**, French St. Martin, ☎ 590-87-75-79.

TELEPHONE:

- *The area code for **French** St. Martin is 590.*
- *The area code for **Dutch** St. Martin is 599.*
- *When calling within the French system, add a 0 to the nine-digit local number (0590-xx-xx-xx).*
- *When calling from the Dutch side to the French side, dial 00, then 590, then 590 again, plus the six-digit number (00-590-590-xx-xx-xx).*
- *When calling from the French side to the Dutch side, dial 00 + 99 + the seven-digit number.*
- *When dialing St. Martin from the US or Canada, dial 011 to get international service, then the area code, 590 for the French side or 599 for the Dutch side, plus the on-island number. When calling a number on the French side, you must dial 590 twice (011-590-590-xx-xx-xx).*
- *When calling the islands from Great Britain, dial 00 to get international service, then the area code, 590 or 599, plus the on-island number, which means you will dial 590 twice when calling the French side (00-590-590-xx-xx-xx).*

TELEPHONE CARDS: Public phone booths don't accept coins. Buy a *Télécarte*, which looks like a credit card, to make local and international calls when you're on the **French** side and a similar-looking **TELCard,** when you're on **Dutch** soil. This is less expensive than phoning from your hotel. TELCards are readily available at convenience stores, gas stations, and hotel desks on the Dutch side. A *Télécarte* may be harder to find on the French side, but most resorts and many shops in the larger towns have them.

St. Martin

Major credit cards can be used from some phone booths on both sides of the island for long distance calls, but the rates are higher than with a prepaid calling card.

Cell Phones make calls from the Dutch to the French side easier and are a less expensive way of calling the US, Europe or neighboring islands. **East Caribbean Cellular** covers St. Martin and St. Barts, ☎ 599-542-2100, www.eastcaribbeancellular.com.

TELEPHONE OPERATOR: ☎ 599-542-2211 on the Dutch side; ☎ 12 on the French side.

TEMPERATURE RANGE: Year-round average low is 72°F and the average high is 86°F.

TIME: Both sides of St. Martin are on Atlantic Standard Time and do not observe Daylight Savings Time. During the summer months, island time is the same as Eastern Daylight Time; in the winter, island time is one hour ahead. St. Martin's time is five hours behind England and six hours behind France and the rest of western Europe during the summer; four hours behind England and five hours behind western Europe in the winter.

TIPPING IN RESTAURANTS: On the Dutch side, a service charge may or may not be added to the bill's total. If one is added, most people leave another 5-10% on the table for the server, since anything added to the bill is split among all the employees.

On the French side, as in France, the service charge is added (hidden) to the price of each item on the menu and divided among the restaurant's employees. Most people leave an additional 5-10% for the waiter in appreciation for good service.

If service is poor, tell the manager or owner as you leave the restaurant. Simply not leaving a tip will do nothing to correct the problem.

TOURIST OFFICES:

Dutch side: Sint Maarten Tourism Office, ☎ 800-786-2278 (in North America), located at W.G. Buncamper Road 33, in the Vineyard Park Building near the Police station on the northeast end of Philipsburg. Local contact, ☎ 599-542-2337, fax 599-542-2734, www.st-maarten.com.

French side: Office du Tourisme de Saint-Martin, located on Route de Sandy-Ground, near the Saint Martin Arawak Museum on the south side of Marigot, ☎ 590-87-57-21, fax 590-87-56-43, www.st-martin.org.

WEBSITES:

Dutch Tourist Office

www.st-maarten.com

French Tourist Office

www.st-martin.org

Other Informative Sites

★www.everythingstmartin.com

www.stmaarten.org

www.sint-maarten.org

WiFi HOTSPOTS: There are many WiFi hotspots, including the Boardwalk in Philipsburg, Sonesta Maho Beach Hotel, Divi Little Bay Resort, Great Bay Beach Resort and Oyster Bay Beach Resort. More businesses and hotels are expected to add hotspots soon.

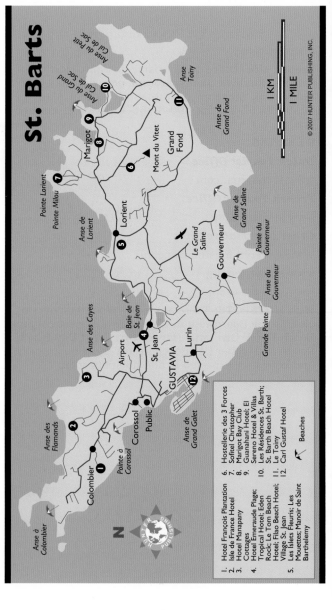

St. Barts

1. Hotel François Plantation
2. Isle de France Hotel
3. Hotel Manapany Cottages
4. Hotel Emeraude Plage; Tropical Hotel; Eden Rock; Le Tom Beach Hotel; Filao Beach Hotel; Village St. Jean
5. Les Islets Fleuris; Les Mouettes; Manoir de Saint Barthelemy
6. Hostellerie des 3 Forces
7. Sofitel Christopher
8. Marigot Bay Club
9. Guanahani Hotel; El Sereno Hotel & Villas
10. Les Résidences St. Barth; St. Barth Beach Hotel
11. Le Toiny
12. Carl Gustaf Hotel

✈ Beaches

© 2007 HUNTER PUBLISHING, INC.

St. Barts

For such a tiny island, measuring only eight square miles, **Saint Barthélemy** (say *sain bar tay leh MEE*) has a mighty reputation and enormous appeal. Fans call it by its diminutive nicknames, St. Barts or St. Barth, which fit its sleek prestigious image better than its long official French name, and

are vastly better than its Columbus-given Italian name, St. Bartoloméo.

The island is probably the least Caribbean of all the Caribbean islands. Since it has little history, it has few remnants of colonial architecture, few residents who trace their ancestry back to African slaves, and few deeply entrenched West Indian traditions. All in all, it's an attractive little enclave that takes great care to protect its privacy and doesn't try in the least to be anything that it is not.

Top Temptations

- **Fabulous little hotels** with distinct personalities.
- **Privacy**, even for celebrities.
- Magnificent **gourmet restaurants**.
- **Chic boutiques**.
- More than 20 **beaches**, some among the best in the Caribbean.
- **Hiking** to hidden coves.
- Villa spying while **cruising** the coast.

Before the late 1960s, St. Barts was an isolated hide-away for the ultra-rich. Fewer than 400 people lived full-time on the island as recently as 1967. Today, the permanent population numbers around 7,000, and the island draws thousands of visitors year-round. Promoters have begun courting a wider range of travelers to fill the expanding number of hotel rooms, but the majority of visitors still are wealthy North Americans, and many of those hold celebrity status.

Don't let St. Barts elitist reputation keep you away. The tiny isle is really quite affable, and while prices are among the highest in the Caribbean, they aren't wildly outside the budget of many travelers, especially during the off-season. You won't have a non-stop schedule of things to do and places to see, but if you're seeking peace, relaxation, and hedonist pleasures, St. Barts offers the best that money can buy.

Like French St. Martin, St. Barts is part of the *sous-préfecture* which is overseen by Guadeloupe, a *département français d'outremer.* Four elected representatives speak for this overseas department in the French *Assemblée Nationale,* and two elected senators hold seats in the *Sénat.* Residents enjoy all the social programs available to French citizens living on the continent, but are heavily dependent on France economically and politically. Residents of Guadeloupe regularly lobby for autonomy, but French St. Martin and St. Barts appear content with their status as French possessions.

 Citizens of St. Barts are French nationals and carry passports issued by the European Union.

Getting There

By Air

Most travelers get to St. Barts via St. Martin. Several major airlines have direct flights to **Queen Juliana International Airport** (SXM) on the Dutch side. You can also take a direct flight to San Juan, Puerto Rico, then hop over to St. Martin on a connecting flight before taking a 15-minute ride on a regional carrier to **Aéroport de St. Jean**, ☎ 590-27-65-41, on St. Barts. In addition, **Air Caraïbes** has service from Guadeloupe.

After you land on St. Martin and go through customs, claim your bags, then walk through the courtyard to the departure terminal, where you will find the check-in counter for all the regional airlines. Get a boarding pass from the airline taking you to St. Barts, then take it and your passport to the brown booth, where you can get a departure tax waiver. You can't get the tax waiver without a boarding pass, and you can't get into the boarding area without your passport, tax waiver, and boarding pass.

St. Barts' Airport (SBH), near St. Jean Bay on the north coast, has one short runway and accepts nothing larger than 20-seat planes. Since there are no runway lights, flights can't land after dark. The recently-enlarged terminal has car rental booths, a small store, and a bar. **La Savane Commercial Center**, just across a narrow road, has a pharmacy, supermarket, and a couple of shops.

Flying to St. Barts is a thrill. Pilots are required to have special training, and you'll understand why once you've seen the landing approach. After takeoff out of St. Martin, your little plane climbs, soars, and almost immediately begins its descent. You get a great low-level view of St. Barts as you approach. Then, about the time you begin to wonder why you don't see the airport, the pilot shoves the plane's nose sharply towards the ground, you glimpse the tops of cars on the road below as you glide by, much too close, then plunge below a mountaintop directly onto the landing strip. Just when you think the plane will hit the ocean at the end of the short runway, you stop.

Wow!

Pilots perform this magic flawlessly several times a day, so the experience is a thrill, not a danger. Later, take a walk along the beach beside the airport and watch this amazing feat from the ground.

You must phone the airport in St. Martin at the following numbers for information.

International Carriers	
Air France	☎ 800-237-2747 (US/Canada), 599-545-4212 (St. Martin), www.airfrance.com
American Airlines/American Eagle	☎ 800-433-7300 (US/Canada), 599-545-2040 (St. Martin), www.aa.com
Continental Airlines	☎ 800-525-0280 (US), 599-545-3444 (St. Martin), www.continental.com
Delta Air Lines	☎ 800-221-1122 (US/Canada), 599-545-2545 (St. Martin), www.delta.com
KLM	☎ 599-545-4747 (St. Martin), 800-374-7747 (US/Canada), www.klm.com
US Airways	☎ 800-428-4322 (US), 599-545-4344 (St. Martin), www.usair.com

Local Airlines & Air Taxis	
St. Barth Commuter	☎ 590-27-54-54, fax 590-27-54-58 (St. Barts), www.stbarthcommuter.com
Winair	☎ 888-975-7888 (US & Canada). 604-272-1174, www.newconcepts.ca

By Inter-Island Ferry

Voyager I and ***Voyager II***, ☎ 599-542-4096 (Philipsburg), 059-87-10-68 (Marigot), 0590-27-54-10 (Gustavia), www.voyager-st-barths.com

The Edge, ☎ 599-544-2640, www.stmaarten-activities.com

Rapid Explorer, ☎ 599-542-9762, www.rapidexplorer.com

You can find additional information about inter-island ferry service on page 42.

Water Taxi

Master Ski Pilou, ☎ 590-27-91-79 or 590-690-61-37-07 (cell) for 24/7 pick-up in a high-speed boat.

Getting Around

Le **Shuttle** has four gray Volkswagon vans that travel two established routes between 9 am and 1 am daily. One bus routinely travels west out of Gustavia to Anse des Flamands and along the north coast as far as Anse des Cayes. The other buses head east from Gustavia toward Anse Toiny. If your destination is not along the designated routes, you may request a special pick-up or drop-off. Round-trip tickets are available at most hotel reception desks and vacation-rental offices, some restaurants and a few boutiques at a cost of €10 (about $12). Unlimited daily passes also are available for three days or more for €10 per day. For information or to request a pick up, call the shuttle office, ☎ 590-29-44-19.

By Taxi

Taxis are plentiful, and fares are generally low, since it's impossible to go very far. They wait at the airport and ferry dock in Gustavia, or you can call the offices in either Gustavia (☎ 590-27-66-31) or St. Jean (☎ 590-27-75-81). Drivers offer sightseeing tours, and most will agree to drop you at a beach and return for you at an appointed time. In addition, you can contact **JC Taxi** for tours or transportation in a new 10-passenger van. ☎ 690-49-02-97, fax 690-29-27-63

Taxis are privately owned and do not have meters, so always agree on a rate before you get into the cab. Drivers charge more on holidays, Sundays, and after dark.

By Rental Car

The best way to get around, even if you're just a day-visitor, is by rental car. The roads are narrow (but in good shape), and you will have to tackle steep inclines and sharp curves. Otherwise, conditions are great: driving is on the right; there's very little traffic outside Gustavia; the island has no traffic lights; the speed limit is 28 mph (45 kph).

The tiny but chic Smart Car is a popular rental, and many people enjoy driving the jeep-like no-doors mini moke, but both are being phased out. You may still be able to find one to rent, but you can also request a larger car with automatic transmission and air conditioning. Don't bother with a four-wheel-drive vehicle. You need a valid driver's license and a credit card to rent a car.

Daily rates run about $60 per day during high season, but drop to around $40 during the off-season. Weekly rates are a better deal at approximately $350 in high season, $245 in low season, depending on the size and condition of the vehicle.

Cars are fuel-efficient, and distances are short, so you won't fill up often, which is good, since there are only **two gas stations** on the island. One is across from the airport in St. Jean, ☎ 590-27-50-50. It's open Monday-Saturday, 7:30 am-noon and 2:30-5 pm; closed Sunday. The other gas station is in Lorient, ☎ 590-27-62-30. It's open daily, 7:30 am-5 pm, except Thursdays, when it closes at noon, and Sundays, when it's closed all day. There is also a 24-hour automatic gas pump at the airport that accepts credit cards.

Reserve your rental car in advance, especially during high season.

Following are local contact numbers. For toll-free numbers and websites, see page 46.

International Car Rental Companies	
Avis	☎ 800-831-2847; St. Jean Airport, 590-27-71-43, fax 590-27-69-32
Budget	☎ 800-472-3325; St. Jean Airport, ☎ 590-27-66-30, fax 590-27-83-93; Gustavia, ☎ 590-27-67-43, fax 590-27-83-93
Europcar	St. Jean Airport, ☎ 590-27-73-33, fax 590-27-80-77
Hertz	St. Jean Airport, ☎ 590-27-71-14, fax 590-27-90-63
Local Car Rental Companies	
Island	St. Jean Airport, ☎ 590-27-70-01, fax 590-27-62-55
Chez Béranger	Gustavia, ☎ 590-27-89-00, fax 590-27-80-28
Gumbs	St. Jean Airport, ☎ 590-27-75-32, fax 590-27-78-99
Questel	St. Jean Airport, ☎ 590-27-73-22, fax 590-27-89-54
Turbe	St. Jean Airport, ☎ 590-27-71-42, fax 590-27-75-57

St. Barts

Getting Married

Honeymooning on St. Bart is fabulous. Getting legally married on the island is a French horror story. Unless you're a citizen of France, forget about it. The requirements, waiting period, and paperwork are just too difficult. But, if you're determined, contact **The French Government Tourist Office** in New York, ☎ 202-659-7779, or the **Office du Tourisme** on St. Barts, ☎ 590-27-87-27, well in advance for advice.

Exploring St. Barts

Taxi Tours

You'll get individual attention and if you take a guided tour with one of the island's delightful taxi drivers. Request an English-speaking driver who knows the island well, and agree on a fee before you start out. You'll pay about $40-$50 for two people on a two-hour tour. Check with the Office du Tourisme for a current list of recommended guides, or contact one of the following:

Raymond Gréaux, ☎ 590-27-66-32

Denis Gumbs, ☎ 590-27-65-61

René Bernier, ☎ 590-27-63-75

Justin Gréaux, ☎ 590-27-62-94

Independent Touring

The very best way to see St. Barts is on your own. Set your own pace, stop when something interests you, and linger as long as you like at outstanding sites. The island is not physically gorgeous overall, as some travel guides would lead you to believe, but it has many, many beautiful places.

St. Barts is shaped like a flaky croissant with both ends pointing north, a puffy middle, and mouse-size bites all along the edges. **Gustavia** is on the southwest outward curve; **St. Jean** is directly over the hilly midsection, nestled into the northwest inward curve. More than 20 coves and beaches are nibbled into the shoreline. Steep, winding roads criss-cross the entire island, and even ace navigators get lost. But, you'll easily find your way again, and you'll discover incredible vistas and sites along the way. St. Barts is no more than two miles across at its widest point and 11 miles long tip-to-tip, so you can't drive far without spotting water. Friendly locals will point you in the right direction, if you become hopelessly confused.

A Walking Tour of Gustavia

Start your tour in the capital and largest town on St. Barts. It's built around a lovely horseshoe-shaped harbor filled with elegant yachts from around the world. Unlike most port cities, Gustavia is seldom overrun by cruise ship passengers.

Stop at the **Office du Tourisme** when you come into town to pick up maps and brochures. It's located on the harborfront at Quai du Général de Gaulle and is open Monday-Friday, 8 am-12:30 pm, and Saturdays, 9-11 am.

You can park in the free lot at Quai du Général de Gaulle, then explore on foot. Everything is laid out on a half-dozen main streets running parallel to the three-sided harbor, and you can easily walk to the shops, sidewalk cafés, a couple of historic sites, and Shell Beach.

 Picture Gustavia as a squared-off capital "U," with the top opening facing northwest. Standing at the bottom of the "U" and facing the harbor, the landside ferry dock and tourist office are on your right. On your left, the waterside arm of the "U" is a peninsula that juts out into the sea. Its far tip is known as La Pointe, location of Wall House and Fort Oscar. Rue Jeanne d'Arc parallels the waterside arm, Rue de la République runs along the landside arm, and Rue du Centenaire connects the two at the bottom of the "U." All of the town's other streets run parallel and perpendicular to these three main roads.

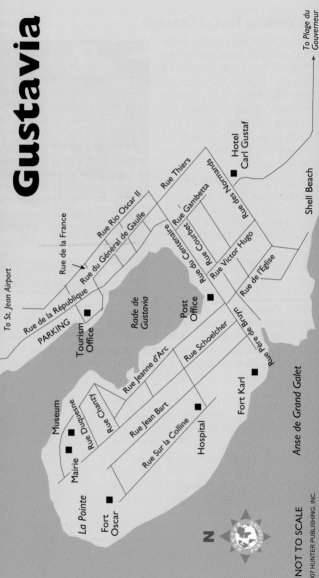

Gustavia

To St. Jean Airport

To Plage du Gouverneur

Rue de la France

Rue Rio Oscar II

Rue du Général de Gaulle

Rue Thiers

Rue Gambetta

Rue Courbet

Rue du Centenaire

Rue Victor Hugo

Rue des Normands

Rue de l'Eglise

Hotel Carl Gustaf

Shell Beach

Rue de la République

PARKING

Tourism Office

Rade de Gustavia

Post Office

Rue Jeanne d'Arc

Rue Schoelcher

Rue Père de Bruyn

Museum

Mairie

Rue Duquesne

Rue Chanzy

Rue Jean Bart

Rue Sur la Colline

Hospital

Fort Karl

La Pointe

Fort Oscar

Anse de Grand Galet

NOT TO SCALE

N

HUNTER PUBLISHING

© 2007 HUNTER PUBLISHING, INC.

The parking lot and its adjoining gazebo are on tree-lined Rue de la République. Attractive two-story colonial-style buildings line the inland side of the road and house some of the island's classy boutiques. Most of the town's original architecture was destroyed during a 1744 British invasion. New structures were built around Le Carénage (as the port was called) and the Swedes added their own styles when they took over in 1785, but most of that was reduced to ashes and rubble by a hurricane and fire in 1852.

Nevertheless, a few lovely old buildings still stand in the capital. The former Swedish governor's home is now the **Mairie**, or town hall, and you can see the green and white *maison* on Rue Auguste Nejman (also spelled Nyman), which is a straight walk inland from the harbor along Rue Couturier.

The Vieux Clocher

The **Vieux Clocher** (old bell tower) doesn't have a bell any more, but the picturesque structure is probably the oldest in town. It was built in 1799 as part of a church on Rue du Presbytère at the southeast end of town, and the elevated bell notified residents as each hour passed throughout the day. A large clock has replaced the original bell, and the church was destroyed long ago, but the lovely stone tower stands as a reminder of the town's colonial past.

On Rue du Centenaire, a handsome street that runs along the harbor's shortest side, you'll find the old **Saint-Barthélemew Anglican church**, topped by a

St. Barts

bell tower and surrounded by a low rock wall. It was built in 1885 with stone from St. Eustatius and France. Services are held here every Sunday at 9 am, ☎ 590-27-89-44.

The **Catholic church**, between Rue du Presbytère and Rue de l'Eglise, is even older. It was built in 1822 in a style similar to the island's oldest Catholic church in Lorient. The bell tower is detached from and taller than the austere main building, which allows the bell to peal more intensely. Masses are held at either the Lorient or Gustavia church on Sundays, 8 am, and Saturdays, 5:30 pm. If you want to attend, call to find out which church will be having services, ☎ 590-27-61-08.

St. Barts Municipal Museum (also called *Musée Municipal, Musée Saint-Barthélemy,* and *Wall House Museum)* is located in an old gray-stone warehouse known locally as **Wall House** on Rue Schoelcher at the far end of La Pointe. It's topped by colorful flags; old cannons sit outside. Inside, you can browse among the photographs, ancient maps, paintings, and artifacts spanning the island's French, British, and Swedish history. Director Eddy Galvani has done a terrific job of recreating the island's past through fascinating displays of ancestral costumes, antique tools, model Créole homes, and traditional fishing boats. Admission is €5 and the museum is open Tuesday-Friday, 8:30 am-12:30 pm, and 2:30-6 pm, Monday, 2:30-6 pm, and Saturday, 9 am-1 pm, ☎ 590-29-71-55.

The Swedes built three defensive forts around the harbor. **Fort Oscar**, which is closed to the public, stands facing the sea on the far side of La Pointe at the end of Rue Jean Bart. Fort Karl has long-since disappeared.

The ruins of **Fort Gustav** are scattered next to the weather station and lighthouse (built in 1961) on the hill at the north end of town. You won't see much history at Fort Gustav, but you can drive there as you leave Gustavia going toward Public. A panoramic tableau identifies neighbor islands and the main buildings in Gustavia. Visit late in the day, and enjoy the glorious view of the town as the sun sets over the ocean.

"Anse" is French for cove or bay. It also means handle, like the anse of a frying pan, which is what many deep bays look like.

Anse de Grand Galet (*galet* is French for pebble), commonly known as **Shell Beach**, is a short walk from Gustavia. Follow Rue Jeanne d'Arc away from town to find the beach, which is covered with thousands of small sea shells brought in by waves. Hurricane Lenny, which made a nasty pass over the island in 1999, caused a lot of damage here, but new sand was brought in to rebuild the beach in the spring of 2000, and shells are washing ashore again. There are better places to sun or swim, but the shells make a nice surface for strolling and jogging. You can see the islands of St. Eustatius and Saba in the distance.

*Sunsets are fantastic from Shell Beach. Stop by at the end of the day, then have dinner at **Dõ Brazil Restaurant**, right on the beach. They specialize in Brazilian and French food, and serve breakfast, lunch, and dinner during high season (call for limited low-season hours), ☎ 590-29-06-66.*

Before you leave Gustavia, wander along the streets and stop at a few of the town's many shops, art galleries, bars, and restaurants. A little **produce market** (*ti marché*) is set up on Rue du Roi Oscar, where ladies from Guadeloupe (locally known as *Doudous*) sell fruits, vegetables and spices from their fertile island. If you've lingered long enough for happy hour, stop for a *ti punch* at one of the well-known people-watching spots such as **Le Select** or **L'Oubli**.

See Where to Eat, *page 213, for restaurant recommendations and* Shopping, *page 190, for information on stores and galleries.*

Along the North Coast

Eden Rock Resort, St. Jean Bay

St. Jean is the island's number two town and its main tourist center. Its spectacular crescent-shaped **Baie de Saint-Jean** is divided by a cliff supporting Eden Rock Resort and has a calm reef-sheltered eastern area and a larger western stretch with more surf. Airplanes take off over the western beach, which is located at the end of the airport's short runway. Watersports operators, restaurants, resorts, and bars line up along the length of the bay.

A favorite pastime is standing on **La Tourmente**, the central hill that separates St. Jean from Gustavia, to watch the planes approach, glide low overhead, then dive below the rise to land. Five shopping malls are home to ritzy boutiques, excellent restaurants, and the only gas station on the island that accepts credit cards; lovely homes dot the surrounding hillsides.

Airport at La Tourmente

Lorient, just east of St. Jean, is a quiet village full of history. The first French settlement was built here in 1648, and the town has two charming cemeteries decorated with crosses and flowers at each grave. It's also home to the island's oldest **Catholic church**, Notre Dame de l'Assomption, where St. Barts Music Festival holds annual performances each January and mass is held at 7 pm on Sundays. One of the island's two gas stations is located here, along with a couple of mini-marts, and a petite post office.

Just past the most eastern cemetery, a road leads to the long white-sand beach, **Anse de Lorient** – popular with surfers. (The annual St. Barth Festival of Caribbean Cinema is held on the tennis courts of the AJOE Surf Club each April.)

 *Look for **Le Manoir** de St. Barthélemy (☎ 590-27-79-27) on Route de Saline near the Ligne St. Barth boutique. It is a Norman house built in 1610 and brought*

in pieces to St. Barts in 1984 by Jeanne Audy Rowland, author of Fils de Vikings *(Viking Sons), a history of St. Barts written in French. The rustic structure was reconstructed on the island and now serves as the centerpiece for the low-budget hotel near Lorient Beach.*

The Coast Road

East of Lorient, the main road veers off toward **Pointe Milou** and **Mont Jean** and becomes dramatic. It winds up the hillsides in this isolated residential area past some of the island's most beautiful homes, villas, and resorts. The coast has no beaches and is covered with rocks that are battered by the pounding surf. Overlooks on top of the sheer cliffs offer spectacular views of nearby islets and faraway St. Martin. Stop for a drink at the **Sofitel Christopher Hotel**, located at the bottom of the steep road leading to Pointe Milou. The bar sits beside an infinity pool that appears to merge with the sea. If the conditions are right, local surfers will be riding the waves offshore.

Anse de Marigot and **Anse du Grand Cul-de-Sac** are attractive lagoons on the far eastern tip of the north coast. The main road climbs, dips, and winds through the hills east of the village of Marigot and passes the calm bays, which are lined with golden sand and surrounded by protective cliffs. Windsurfers take advantage of the steady breeze, swimmers float in the deep blue placid water, and snorkelers enjoy exploring the close-in reefs.

Watersports operators rent all types of equipment (including the popular kitesurfers) and restaurants, bars, and resorts provide all the creature comforts. The terrain in this area is quite arid, but the hotels have planted palms and bushes along their stretches of beach, and the resorts' gardens are colorful and lush.

Morne du Vitet is the island's highest peak at 922 feet. Its steep slopes are criss-crossed by low stone walls that once imprisoned sheep and goats. Drive up the mountain's winding narrow road that goes south from Grand Cul-de-Sac for panoramic views of the rugged coastline.

Anse des Cayes, Anse des Lézards, Anse des Flamands and **Petite Anse** line up along the northern shore west of the town of St. Jean. Surfers favor Cayes and Lézards, while swimmers and snorkelers prefer Flamands and Petite Anse. Each is worth a visit. Although the beaches are adjacent to one another, they are separated by rocky outcroppings, which prevent you from walking from one to the other.

Ile Fourchue

This uninhabited island off the western coast is a popular day-trip from St. Barts. Visitors like to go out to the tiny isle to get away from civilization, explore the rocky desert-like terrain, and climb to the top of the hills for extraordinary views. The entire place is a nature preserve and underwater life is protected by the St. Bart Marine Reserve. Forty-two of the 54 coral species known to thrive in the Lesser Antilles grow off-shore, and a vast number of sea creatures live around the reefs. If you decide to visit, you'll have only wild goats for company, and there's no shade, so plan accordingly. Expect to pay about $100 per person for a scheduled day cruise, snorkeling equipment, open bar, and a gourmet lunch with wine. Contact the following for information: **Marine Service**, Quai du Yacht Club, Gustavia, ☎ 590-27-70-34; **Yacht Charter Agency**, Rue Jeanne d'Arc, Gustavia, ☎ 590-27-62-38; **Océan Must**, La Pointe, near Wall House, Gustavia, ☎ 590-27-62-25. Beware of seasickness if the ocean is rough or you're prone to that type of malady.

West of Gustavia

Anse de Colombier is one of the most spectacular sites on the island, and the only way to get there is by boat or on foot. Two hiking paths lead to the secluded beach; one begins at the top of the hill above the waterfront; the other begins near Petite Anse, on the Atlantic coast northwest of Anse des Flamands. Either trek will take about 20 to 30 minutes.

The hilltop path starts near a rock lookout point in a parking lot at the end of a paved road west of the tiny village of **Colombier**. (An orientation tableau points out little nearby isles and St. Martin in the distance.) The trail is steep, rocky, lined with cactus, and a real challenge for anyone in less than top physical shape. If you can make it down, you'll find it less difficult going back up, since you'll have better traction, thus less slipping.

The path from Petite Anse is lovely and less taxing. It's nothing more than an old goat path at the end of the paved road from Flamands that goes all the way to the west end of the island, then curves southward. Steps lead down to Anse du Colombier. You won't have much climbing, since there are only gradual changes in elevation, and several points along the rocky, winding trail have spectacular views.

St. Barts

No matter which trail you take, wear closed-toe shoes and bring water. There's no shade and no facilities once you reach the sand at Anse de Colombier. And don't expect to be alone. Private yachts and tour boats from Gustavia stop here, and you will probably not be the only one to hike in. The water is usually calm and ideal for swimming and snorkeling; the long crescent-shaped beach has deep white sand and a view of St. Martin.

Colombier is nothing more than a small village with a chapel built in 1918, a school, a few shops, and hillside homes for about 300 residents. Visit for the dramatic views of Anse Colombier and Anse des Flamands.

 *You can drive to the village of **Colombier** on a very steep paved road that begins in the center of the little village of **Flamands**.*

Corossol, on the south coast west of Gustavia, is a traditional fishing village with fewer than 300 residents living in colorful houses topped by orange-red roofs. Some of the local women still weave hats and baskets from the leaves of palm trees and sell them from their little wooden cottages, which are called *cases* (say *caz*).

🌶 *Traditional houses on St. Barts are either* les cases à vent *(wind houses), which are built to withstand hurricane-force gales, or* les cases Créoles *(Créole houses),* which are constructed to provide shade and ventilation. Both types have free-standing kitchens so heat from cooking won't come into the living areas and an accidental fire won't burn down the entire home.

Brightly painted fishing boats float on the calm turquoise waters of **Anse de Corossol**, and lobster traps lie along the beige-sand beach. Nearby, **The Inter-Ocean Museum** displays 9,000 seashells from around the world, including 1,600 from the Caribbean. Ingénu Magras owns the private collection and welcomes visitors Tuesday-Sunday, 9 am-12:30 pm and 2-5 pm, ☎ 590-27-62-97. Admission is $5 for adults.

Along the Southeastern Coast

 The beaches at this end of the island are fabulous, but not good for swimming.

Anse du Gouverneur is a long, uncrowded, U-shaped beach at the bottom of an exhilarating mountain road that leads from the small residential village of **Lurin**. The sand is wide, deep, and white, and there's just enough surf to make things interesting. Snorkeling is good around the cliffs at each end, but there are no facilities, and little shade.

 It's rumored that the pirate known as **Montbars the Exterminator** *buried treasure here and never returned for it. Wouldn't hurt to bring a metal detector.*

Looking down on Anse du Gouverneur

Go back to the main road and head east, following the signs for **Grande Saline**. You'll pass the old salt pond, which is now a huge murky basin surrounded by a m a n g r o v e swamp that attracts a lot of tropical birds. Park near the salt pond and walk up the rough trail that leads to a sand dune, where you'll have an awesome view of the sea and Anse de Grande Saline.

Anse de Grande Saline is as lovely as Gouverneur and popular with locals as well as tourists. The white-sand beach is long; rocky cliffs on each end draw a variety of fish, which makes for good snorkeling. Since there are no facilities, you won't have to share your space with a crowd, just a few nude sunbathers.

Anse à Toiny and **Anse Grand Fond** are part of St. Barts' craggy, wild southern coast. Steep cliffs surround both coral beaches and the currents and waves are often too rough for swimmers. Visit for the breath-

Anse à Toiny

taking views and rustic tranquility. You'll probably be entertained by experienced surfers riding the waves.

The Washing Machine is a natural pool hidden in the hills. Get there on foot by following a path from the beach at Grand Fond; about a 10-minute walk. Local surfers favor this secret spot because the swirling agitation caused by seawater pouring into the basin creates impressive breakers.

Anse du Petit Cul-de-Sac is lined with seagrape trees, which provide some shade, and has no development. It's perfect for beach bums who want to get away from it all. The shore is rocky, so not a good place for swimming, but the views are nice, and you'll probably have the whole place to yourself, especially on weekdays. Explore the little caves among the boulders.

Adventures on Water

Best Beaches

The folks who do the official counting say St. Barts has 22 beaches; 15 are suitable for swimming. Even the mathematically challenged can understand that this is an amazing number for an eight-square-mile island.

In the Caribbean, trade winds blow from east to west and on St. Barts the beaches are divided into those on the eastern windward side (*côte au vent*), and those on the western leeward side (*côte sous le vent*). Some of the windward beaches are protected by hills or reefs, so their waters are still ideal for swimming, even though the wind is strong enough for windsurfing. The leeward beaches are protected by the island itself, so their waters are typically calm. Sunset watchers, boaters, and strollers gravitate toward secluded coves where boulders, pebbles, and seashells frustrate swimmers and watersports enthusiasts.

So, which beaches are best? That depends on your intent.

All beaches are public and free, even if a resort is hogging most of the sand. None are officially nude, but topless swimming and sunbathing is common on all of them, and some are known as popular spots for naturalists. We haven't heard of officials hassling anyone for being naked on a public beach here, but it could happen, so best stick to remote spots if you want to strip bare.

Best Beaches on the Windward Side

St. Jean Beach is extremely popular and offers watersports and several bars and restaurants. Nice resorts open directly onto the sand. You can find some natural  ral shade or rent an umbrella. The water is typically calm enough for swimming, and the wind blows strongly enough for windsurfing on the east side of Eden Rock Resort.

Lorient Beach is long and wide and offers some shade. Surfers with their own equipment gather at the eastern end, but families with kids find calm swimming conditions west of mid-beach. You'll have less company here than at St. Jean. The nearby village has restaurants and shops.

Grand Cul-de-Sac has a watersports outfitter (**Wind Wave Power**, ☎ 590-27-82-57) and several places to eat. The long stretch of sand is narrow and protected by an offshore reef.

Anse Toiny is for the experienced surfer and beach stroller. The currents are too strong for swimming, but you'll love this wild, remote part of the island.

Anse de Grande Saline is dazzling. Do not miss its unspoiled grandeur. The only drawback is the lack of shade, which doesn't seem to bother the nude sunbathers.

Best Beaches on the Leeward Side

Anse du Gouverneur has tons of great sand, calm water, and no facilities. It's perfect for lounging, swimming, and snorkeling. You may have a lot of company, but it's just as likely you'll have the whole place to yourself. Bring sunblock or an umbrella because there's no natural shade.

Anse de Colombier (Don West)

Anse de Colombier is a fabulous off-the-beaten-track beach that can be reached only by boat or on foot. Two old goat paths lead to the gorgeous sand surrounded by green hills. One begins from a parking lot at the end of the main road that cuts through the village of Colombier;

the other leaves from Petite Anse, at the end of the paved road from Flamands. The trail from Petite Anse is less difficult. Bring drinks and snacks, since you'll want to stay awhile. The water is ideal for swimming and snorkeling.

Anse des Flamands (Don West)

Anse des Flamands is a long, wide, lovely beach with fine sand. Palms provide shade for afternoon naps, and sometimes the waves kick up enough for body surfing. Park in the lot beside the Grande Saline salt pond (a smelly, marshy place favored by tropical birds) and walk down a dirt road, over a rocky rise and a sand dune, to the gorgeous turquoise water. Ile Chevreaux, a small offshore isle, is straight out from the white sand beach.

 Author's tip: *Marigot Bay and Petit Cul de Sac, both on the northeast side, are less-visited small beaches that are favored by locals.*

Anse des Flamands, left, and La Petite Anse (Don West)

Jet Skiing & Water-Skiing

The following organize Jet Ski tours of the coast and rent equipment to individuals. Tour costs are in the $60-$80 range, depending on the length of the trip. Jet skis rent for about $50 per half-hour. **Master Ski Pilou** and **Marine Services** also offer water-skiing trips priced in the $55 range.

 Use of motorized watersports equipment is prohibited within 300 yards of the shore.

Master Ski Pilou, Carl Gustaf Resort, Gustavia, ☎ 590-27-91-79, cell 690-61-37-07

Wind Wave Power, Saint-Barth Beach Hotel, Grand Cul-de-Sac, ☎ 590-27-82-57, fax 590-27-72-76

Marine Service, Quai du Yacht Club, Gustavia, ☎ 590-27-70-34, fax 590-27-70-36. Ask for Stéphan Jouany, an expert water-skier.

Surfboarding, Kiteboarding & Windsurfing

When the surf's up, all the surfer dudes head for Lorient, Toiny, St. Jean, Pointe Milou, or Grand Cul-de-Sac. Rent a board from one of the following outfitters for about $20 per hour.

St. Barts Waterplay, St. Jean Beach, ☎ 690-61-38-40

Reefers Surf Club, Lorient, ☎ 590-27-54-15

Sea Sports Club, Eden Rock Resort, St. Jean, ☎ 590-27-74-77, fax 590-27-88-37

Wind Wave Power, Saint-Barth Beach Hotel, Grand Cul-de-Sac, ☎ 590-27-82-57, fax 590-27-72-76

Surf Life Creation, Pointe Milou, ☎ 590-27-94-64

Kite Surf School, Gran Cul-de-Sac & St. Jean Beach, ☎ 690-69-26-90

Boating

St. Barts is a yacht haven. If you don't own your own boat, rent one for the day or week, or join a scheduled sightseeing/snorkeling/sunset cruise. Prices vary according the type of boat, length of trip, and included extras, so check with a couple of companies listed below to compare your options. We found full-day cruises running about $100 per person, including snorkeling, open bar, lunch, and two beach stops. The Yellow Submarine semi-submersible tour costs $60 for adults and $20 for children.

Several boating events take place on the island each year, including the **Saint-Barth Regatta** in February, the **Saint-Barth's Cup** in April, and the **International Regatta** in May. Contact the Office du Tourisme, ☎ 590-27-87-27, or the **Saint Barth Yacht Club**, ☎ 590-27-70-41, for exact dates and information.

Marine Service, Quai du Yacht Club, Gustavia, ☎ 590-27-70-34, fax 590-27-70-36

Nautica, Rue de la République, Gustavia, ☎ 590-27-56-50, fax 590-27-56-52

Caraïbes Yachting, Rue Jeanne d'Arc, Gustavia, ☎ 590-590-27-52-06

St. Barts

Océan Must, La Pointe, Gustavia, ☎ 590-27-62-25; 590-27-95-17

Yannis Marine, Gustavia, Rue Jeanne d'Arc, ☎ 590-29-89-12, 690-59-01-51 (cell), www.yannismarine.com

Yellow Submarine, Gustavia Harbour, ☎ 590-52-40-51

Deep-Sea Fishing

Anglers head to the waters off Lorient, Flamands, and Corossol to reel in tuna, marlin, bonito, barracuda, and wahoo. Several local big-game anglers will take your party out on a private excursion or hook you up with another group. Costs are about $450 per day or $300 per half-day for a group of four, but the prices vary widely depending on the number in your group, size of the boat, and type of gear, food, and drinks supplied.

Ocean Must, La Pointe, Gustavia, ☎ 590-27-62-25, fax 590-27-95-17

Marine Service, Quai du Yacht Club, Gustavia, ☎ 590-27-70-34, fax 590-27-70-36

Capitaine Patrick La Place, ☎ 590-27-61-76, 690-59-15-87 (cell)

Yannis Marine, Gustavia, Rue Jeanne d'Arc, ☎ 590-29-89-12, 690-59-01-51 (cell), www.yannismarine.com

Boat Rental St. Barth, Gustavia, ☎ 690-30-58-73, www.boatrentalsstbarth.com

Adventures Underwater

The ocean surrounding St. Barts is full of marine life and pristine coral reefs protected as a marine park since 1996. Most guides take divers to sites near Gustavia where caves and a wreck provide interesting swim-throughs. Anemones, urchins, sea cucumbers and eels live on the reefs along with turtles, conch and many species of tropical fish. Most of the reefs are in fairly shallow water and offer good visibility.

Contact one of the following dive operators to schedule a scuba trip. Costs range from $90 for a one-tank dive to $150 for a two-tank dive. Multi-day packages are also available.

La Bulle, which is associated with *Ocean Must*, is another major dive operation in Gustavia. Laurence and Fred are PADI-certified instructor/guides who take divers out at 8:30 am, 10:30 am, and 2:30 pm. Their expertise ranges from instructing new students to leading experienced divers on personalized trips to the most challenging sites. Give them a call at the office on La Pointe in the capital (the phone is answered 24 hours a day), ☎ 590-27-62-25 or 590-27-68-93.

Plongée Caraïbes is run by Marion, Franck, and Vincent, three of the friendliest scuba guides on the island. They dive from a huge 46-foot customized catamaran that allows plenty of room, easy-in/easy-out water access, and shade for those who want it. There's even a toilet and hot-water shower. An onboard compressor allows the crew to refill tanks without returning to the dock. The boat goes out at 9:30 am and 2:30 pm daily and every Thursday at 6:30 pm for a night dive. Look for them near the tourist office at the harbor in Gustavia or contact them at ☎ 690-54-66-14 (cell), fax 590-27-55-94, www.plongee-caraibes.com

 St. Barts joined other Caribbean islands in an attempt to protect their marine resources by creating the St. Barths' Marine Reserve on October 10, 1996. Call for additional diving information, ☎ *590-27-88-18.*

Ouanalao Dive gets its name from an ancient Arawak word meaning pelican, which is what Caribbean natives called St. Barts before Colombus renamed it in honor of his brother Bartoloméo in 1493. Today, the

St. Barts

name serves this dive company well. They offer PADI and ANMP certification and a whole range of organized underwater excursions, including drift and night dives. For variety, the bilingual staff can guide you on underwater scooter trips and take you kite surfing. Look for their boat at Sereno Beach Hotel or call to reserve your spot on one of the scheduled daily dives, ☎ 590-27-61-37.

St. Barth Plongée, at Anse des Cayes, is run by the spirited Bertrand Caizergues, better known as Birdy. Over the years, he's taken many satisfied visitors to glorious dive sites in his 28-foot customized boat that's powered by quiet, low-pollution, high-horse-power engines. Only eight divers are allowed per trip, and all equipment is top-of-the-line. Set up a dive by phone, ☎ 590-27-54-44.

Adventures on Land

Horseback Riding

Seeing the island on horseback is fun, even if you don't know anything about riding. Laure Nicolas at Ranch des Flamands, located on a hill above Anse des Flamands beach, organizes two-hour beach and countryside rides each morning at nine o'clock and every afternoon at three o'clock for novice and experienced riders. The cost is $50 per person. **Ranch des Flamands**, Main Road, Flamands, ☎ 590-27-80-72 or 690-62-99-30 (cell), fax 590-52-05-58.

Hiking

Most of St. Barts is hilly, but there are no high mountains to climb, so most hiking is moderately strenuous. If you're in relatively good physical shape, you will enjoy walking along the sandy beaches and hiking the trails that cut across the island's interior countryside.

If you want to trek over some interesting terrain to get to a secluded beach, check with the tourist office (☎ 590-27-87-27) on the Gustavia harbor for trail suggestions.

Le Chemin Douanier (the customs officer's road) is one of the most popular routes. It begins on the pebbly beach at Anse de Grand Fond on the southeast coast and continues into the surrounding hills. You'll see the path at the east end of the beach and follow it past the surfers' favored spot, Washing Machine, until the trail becomes overgrown as it goes uphill. Count on about 45 minutes to walk the path one-way without stopping. You'll probably want to take breaks in the most scenic areas, so allow an additional two or three hours for exploring and resting.

The walk to **Colombier Beach** is spectacular. There are two paths, one from the end of the road that cuts through the village of Colombier and one from the end of the road that goes through the hamlet of Flamands.

St. Barts

Tennis

Tennis buffs will want to stay at one of the resorts with courts, but if you just want to play a couple of times during your vacation, you can pay a guest fee and play at one of the island's tennis clubs. Resorts with courts include Hotel St. Barth Isle de France, Hotel Guanahani, and Hotel Manapany. See *Where to Stay*, page 196, for information and contact numbers for the resorts.

The following tennis clubs welcome visitors and have lighted courts for night play.

Tennis Club du Flamboyant, Grand Cul-de-Sac, ☎ 590-27-69-82

AJOE Tennis Club, Orient, ☎ 590-27-67-63

ASCCO, Colombier, ☎ 590-27-61-07

For private lesson and games, contact French pro **Patrick Sellez**, ☎ 690-35-58-86

Biking

Cycling on St. Barts is easy and fun because of the flat terrain and light traffic. Rent a Trek hybrid for an hour or a month at **Sun Velo**, ☎ 590-87-1856.

Exercise Facilities & Spa Services

Many resorts offer some type of gym equipment and basic massage/facial services, but for a full workout or top-of-the-line beauty treatments, try the following:

Forma Form Fitness, on the main road in Lurin, offers temporary memberships. Once inside the two-story, air-conditioned, glass-walled building, you can run on the track and use the 22 cardiovascular machines and 40 weight machines, or take an aerobics class. Personal trainers also are available for private instruction at an additional fee. The center is open Monday-Saturday 7:30 am-8 pm, Sunday 9 am-noon, ☎ 590-27-51-23.

Shopping

Ardent shoppers will want to stop in Marigot or Philipsburg on St. Martin for the best variety of duty-free merchandise, but St. Barts has many lovely shops. As with everything else on the island, the boutiques are upscale and carry top-quality goods. Most of the best stores are located in Gustavia along Rue du Général de Gaulle and Rue de la République, but St. Jean also has its share of treasures. Since there are more than 200 retail shops on St. Barts, you probably won't get to all of them, so we've sorted through the offerings and present our personal favorites below.

> *Store hours on St. Barts are similar to those in France, with most opening from 8 am until noon, closing during midday for a leisurely déjeuner, then reopening from 2 until 6 pm. Most shops are closed all day Sunday, and some reduce their hours during low season and close for several weeks during the late summer. Call the stores directly to check their hours.*

Top Shops

Jewelry

Fabienne Miot, Rue de la République, Gustavia,
☎ 590-27-73-13

Stop in to see Fabienne's fabulous creations, including the ultimate souvenir, her limited-edition 18-karat gold Medallion of St-Barts. You can watch the artist as she crafts unusually shaped rings, bracelets, and necklaces from pearls, precious stones, and gold.

Diamond Genesis, 12 Rue du Général de Gaulle, ☎ 590-27-66-94

As at Fabienne Miot's shop, jewelry is made right on the premises at Diamond Genesis. There's a little bit of everything here, including big-dollar European-style necklaces and rings, but you can also find some well-priced pieces. Diamonds are, of course, hot sellers, but the shop also sells a huge assortment of watches by international companies such as Jaeger Lecoultre, Tag Heuer, Corum, and Ikepod.

Donna del Sol, Rue de la République, Gustavia,
☎ 590-27-90-53

Even if you don't buy anything, stop by this shop in the Carre d'Or shopping plaza across from the harbor to see the collection of stretch 18K gold bracelets. Each bracelet is made up of three to six rows of thin flexible gold set with diamonds and other precious or semi-precious stones.

Perfume & Cosmetics

Privilège, Rue de la République, Gustavia, ☎ 590-27-67-43; Les Galeries du Commerce, St. Jean, ☎ 590-27-72-08

These sister stores stock so many brand name cosmetics and perfumes, you're sure to find your favorites. Bring an extra bag to tote home your tax-free Chanel, Valmont, Clarins, Christian Dior, Calvin Klein, Hermès....

Skin Care

The Brins family owns and operates **Ligne St. Barth**, the renowned skin care company whose products are used by women throughout the world. Their ancestors came to St. Barts from France in the 1600s, and today the family formulates and manufactures beauty products in the village of Lorient for international distribution. You can visit the store on Route de Saline to purchase skin creams, sun screens, body lotions, and bath oils.

To pamper your skin while you're on the island, consider using their sun screen made from ground *roucou* seeds, which contain a form of vitamin A that stimulates melanin to accelerate tanning. In addition to this ingredient that was first used by the island's Indian inhabitants, the product contains micro-fine zinc oxide to protect your skin from the intense Caribbean sun. Their other products are great island-made gifts for the folks back home. For more information, ☎ 590-27-82-63, www.lignestbarth.com.

Clothing

Shopping centers to look for: **Villa Créole** is on St. Jean's main road east of Eden Rock Resort, in the direction of Grande Saline. **Les Galeries du Commerce** is on the main road between the airport and St. Jean Beach. **La Savanne** is a small complex across the main road from the airport.

Pati de Saint Barth, Villa Créole, St. Jean, ☎ 590-27-59-06, www.patidestbarth.com.

The shops are full of items displaying the popular "St Barth French West Indies" and "Pati de St. Barth" logos, designed by artist and shop owner Pati Guyot.

Terra St. Barths, Centre Pelican, St. Jean Beach, ☎ 590-27-57-50

Wonderful accessories make this clothing store unique. It's located next to the popular beach, so stop in to browse through the hats, bags, and colorful jewelry. The lightweight shawls are perfect for throwing over your shoulders on a balmy St. Barts evening.

Blue Coast, 5 Rue du Bord de Mer, Gustavia, ☎ 590-29-60-18

St. Barts

Owner Marine has filled her little shop with shirts made of fine Irish linen and available in 20 tropical colors. Women have limited selection here, but there's no rule that prohibits them from wearing these soft, pastel men's shirts.

Human Steps, Rue de la France, Gustavia, ☎ 590-27-8557, www.human-steps.com

Both men and women can pick up the latest styles of their favorite shoes here. Look for name brands such as Prada, Miu Miu, Sergio Rossi, Charles Jourdan, Robert Clergerie, and Paul Smith.

Liquor & Wine

Bacchus Boutique, Rue du Bord de Mer, Gustavia, ☎ 590-52-20-96

With sister shops in St. Martin and Anguilla (called Vinissimo), Bacchus is a well-known name among wine connoisseurs. They offer about 400,000 bottles of wine, from simple table varieties to distinguished vintages. The wine waiters are friendly, knowledgeable and eager to help you select the proper bottle for any meal or occasion.

Le Goût du Vin, Rue du Roi Oscar II, Gustavia, ☎ 590-27-88-02

Residents have become accustomed to shopping at this wine and spirit store over the past few years. It's the exclusive distributor of Laurent Perrier Champagnes and wine produced by Bouchard Père et Fils Burgundy, but also stocks an impressive list of Italian, Chilean, Australian, and Spanish wines. Prices range from $5 to $700 per bottle. If you're overwhelmed by the choices, just ask one of the amicable sales staff for help.

La Cave de Saint Barthélemy, Marigot, ☎ 590-27-63-21

The largest (in area) wine cellar on St. Barts (and probably the largest anywhere in the Caribbean), isn't in Gustavia, but in the little town of Marigot. It has 300 varieties of French wine among its 250,000 bottles stored in a 6,000-square-foot climate-controlled area. Closed Sunday and Monday, and from noon until 2 pm, Tuesday-Saturday.

Gifts & Home Decor

The House, Rue du Général de Gaulle, Gustavia, ☎ 590-29-21-14

Walking through the door of this fabulously decorated showroom is like visiting a luxurious private home, only better. Everything is paired up and arranged so that you can see how each piece of furniture and accent object works in a room. Whatever your style, you'll find antiques, replicas, and exquisite accent pieces to carry back to your own house.

Made in St. Barth, Villa Créole, St. Jean, ☎ 590-27-56-57

You can't walk past this red-roofed shop in St. Jean without looking through the window and being drawn into the wonderland of handmade crafts, jewelry, and paintings. Pick up a straw hat made by the women who live in the little village of Corossol, and buy a few Made in St-Barth logo T-shirts for friends back home.

Author's tip: *Drugstore des Caribees is not a pharmacy. The well-stocked shop at Villa Créole in St. Jean offers sunscreen lotions by "Ligne St. Barth," sunglasses, swimsuits and more. Stop in before you hit the beach.* ☎ *590-27-68-20.*

Books, Magazines & Newspapers

Funny Face Books, Carré d'Or, Gustavia, ☎ 590-29-60-14, www.funny-face-books.com

Look for this fine shop on the upper level of this luxury shopping center, above Black Swan and Chopard Boutiques. The owner, Susan Irace, stocks a wide variety of English-language books, along with magazines and newspapers from the US and Britain. You will feel free to browse as long as you want and can also enjoy a cup of coffee or tea. Check out the selection of unique note cards and stationery before you leave.

Groceries

Match Supermarché, La Savane, St. Jean, ☎ 590-27-68-16

Health Products

Pharmacie St. Barth, Rue de la République, Gustavia, ☎ 590-27-61-82

Conveniently located diagonally across from the ferry dock, this drugstore carries all sorts of medicines, over-the-counter cures, herbs, and beauty potions. The friendly staff will help you find exactly what you need, whether you're ill or just hoping to block the damaging rays of the Caribbean sun.

 Author's tip: *You will also find a pharmacy in St. Jean, on the main road, across from the airport.* ☎ *590-27-66-61.*

Art

The Caribbean can make an artist out of almost anyone, and St. Barts draws new talent every year. Many display and sell their art from their home studios or one of the island's galleries. It's impossible to name all the current artists and locations where you can see their work because new names are added constantly while others move on.

Table-à-l'Ombre, by Paul Elliott Thuleau

Look for the following galleries and home studios as you tour the island:

Les Artisans, Artist and jeweler, Alain le Chatelier, Rue du Roi Oscar II, Gustavia, ☎ 590-27-50-40

Galerie Christian Mas, Rue Jeanne d'Arc, Gustavia, ☎ 590-52-93-66

Cargo, Various artists, Villa Créole, St. Jean, ☎ 590-29-84-91

To B. Art Galerie, Le Carré d'Or, Gustavia, ☎ 690-46-66-56 (cell)

Where to Stay

Private Villas

If you really want to do St. Barts right, rent a private villa. All the celebrities do, and you can find exquisite places that are just a bit of a splurge, especially if you share the space and cost with friends. Of course, the most divine abodes are quite pricey, but you can save a little by preparing your own meals and having happy hour on the terrace.

Many rentals include daily maid service, as well as pool and garden maintenance. You can even arrange for a local chef to create scrumptious meals right in your own kitchen. (Try **Cordon Bleu**, ☎ 690-58-78-98.) The best amenity is total privacy. The biggest drawback is that few villas are on a beach, although most have a private pool.

If you decide that villa life is for you, you won't have any problem finding a place. Wee St. Barts has about 400 rentals, and most have more than one bedroom. Expect a just-ok one-bedroom to run about $1,000 per week and a super-luxurious three-or-more-bedroom to top out at more than $30,000 per week. Between these extremes, you'll find many choices that average $4,000 per week per bedroom during high season and about $2,500 per week per bedroom during low season.

 Whether you're reserving a villa or resort room, be aware that everything books up early for the Christmas season. A year is not too early to make reservations; six months is probably too late.

Rental Agencies

★★★St. Barth Properties

☎ 800-421-3396 or 508-527-7727 (US), 590-29-75-05 (St. Barts),
www.stbarth.com

 AUTHOR'S CHOICE American owner Peg Walsh and her staff personally inspect all the villas and preferred hotels that they represent on St. Barts. Stop by the office at Espace du Centenaire in Gustavia or call the US office for a list of properties.

French Caribbean International

☎ 800-322-2223, www.frenchcaribbean.com

Based in California, this rental agency handles hundreds of private villas on all the French Caribbean islands. In addition, the staff has first-hand experience and contact with the island's best hotels.

★Ici et La

☎ 590-27-78-78, fax 590-27-78-28, www.icietlavillas. com

Director Patrick Catalan operates out of an office above the Cartier jewelry store in Gustavia. He and his staff manage properties for absent owners and arrange a variety of services for their villa renters.

Saint Barth V.I.P

Rue de la République, Gustavia

☎ 590-27-94-86, fax 590-27-56-52, www.st-barth-vip.com

V.I.P. stands for Villas in Paradise. This agency is small enough to offer individual services on villas of all sizes.

Resorts & Hotels

St. Barts has some of the most stunning resorts in all of the Caribbean. You won't find high-rise compounds with glitzy casinos and non-stop activities. Rather, you will be

HOTEL PRICE CHART	
For a double room for two	
$	under $300
$$	$300-$400
$$$	$401-$550
$$$$	over $550

nestled into a petit retreat with a dozen or so rooms. (The largest hotel on the island, Hotel Guanahani, has 75 rooms.)

The island has a handful of hotels offering *less expensive* rooms, but don't expect *inexpensive* accommodations. You'll pay about $500 per room per night during "the season" (mid-December through mid-April) and a bit more than half that during the summer and fall. The island is Frenchly blunt about its desire to keep out undesirables and locals have no plans to compromise their standards in order to draw more tourists.

French Stars

Many hotels, restaurants, and shops close annually during late summer and early fall. You may be able to wrangle a great rate at a hotel or private villa during this time, but the island will be very quiet and you will have limited services.

The following scale indicates rates charged per night for a standard double room with two adults during high season. All prices are given in US dollars. Most hotels do not add service charges and there is no hotel tax on St. Barts.

Calling for Reservations

When dialing St. Barts from the US or Canada, dial 011 to get international service, then the area code, **590**, plus the on-island nine-digit number, which means dialing 590 twice (011-590-590-xx-xx-xx).

When calling the islands from Great Britain, dial **00** to get international service, then the area code, **590**, plus the on-island nine-digit number; so you dial 590 twice (00-590-590-xx-xx-xx). On St. Barts or from French St. Martin, you add a **0** to the nine-digit local number (0590-xx-xx-xx).

Accommodations Directory

GUSTAVIA

Carl Gustaf, Rue des Normands, ☎ 590-29-79-00, fax 590-27-82-37, www.hotelcarlgustaf.com, $$$$

ST. JEAN

Eden Rock, St. Jean Beach, ☎ 877-563-7105 (US), 590-29-79-99, fax 590-27-88-37, www.edenrockhotel.com, $$$$

St. Barts

Hôtel Emeraude Plage, St. Jean Beach, ☎ 590-27-64-78; fax 590-27-83-08, www.emeraudeplage.com, $$$

Hôtel les Islets de la Plage, St. Jean Beach, ☎ 590-27-88-57, fax 590-27-88-58, www.lesislets.com, $$$$

Le Village St. Jean, Hillside above St. Jean Bay, ☎ 590-27-61-39, fax 590-27-77-96, www.villagestjeanhotel.com, $$

Tom Beach Hôtel, St. Jean Beach, ☎ 590-27-53-13, fax 590-27-53-15, www.tombeach.com, $$

Tropical Hotel, Hillside above St. Jean Bay, ☎ 590-27-64-87, fax 590-27-81-74, www.tropical-hotel.com, $$

ANSE DU GRAND CUL-DE-SAC

Hôtel les Ondines sur la Plage, ☎ 590-27-69-64, fax 590-52-24-41, $$

Le Guanahani, ☎ 590-27-66-60, fax 590-27-70-70, www.leguanahani.com, $$$$

Le Sereno, ☎ 590-27-64-80, fax 590-29-83-00, www.lesereno.com, $$$$

St. Barth Beach Hotel, ☎ 888-790-5264 (US & Canada), 590-27-60-70, fax 590-27-75-57, www.stbarthbeachhotel.com,

AROUND THE ISLAND

La Banane, Lorient Hills, ☎ 590-52-03-00, fax 590-27-68-44, www.labanane.com, $$$$

Hostellerie des Trois Forces, More Vivet, ☎ 590-27-61-25, fax 590-27-81-38, www.3forces.net, $

Hôtel Manapany, Anse des Cayes, ☎ 800-847-4249 (in the US and Canada) or 590-27-66-55, fax 590-27-75-28, www.lemanapany.com, $$$$

Hôtel St. Barth Isle de France, Baie des Flamands, ☎ 800-810-4691 (US), 590-27-61-81, fax 590-27-86-83, www.isle-de-france.com, $$$$

Le Toiny, Anse de Toiny, ☎ 800-278-6469 (in the US) or 590-27-88-88, fax 590-27-89-30, www.hotelletoiny.com, $$$$

Christopher, Pointe Milou, ☎ 866-287-8017 (US), 590-27-63-63, fax 590-27-92-92, $$$$

In Gustavia

★★Carl Gustaf

Rue des Normands

☎ 590-29-79-00, fax 590-27-82-37
www.hotelcarlgustaf.com

14 one- and two-bedroom suites

$$$$

St. Barts

Set in a hillside garden overlooking the town, this ul-
tra-chic hotel is elegant enough for the Swedish king
whose name it bears. We're talking Italian marble,
Greek columns, private plunge pools, and priceless
sunset views. Each room is decked out in exquisite
furniture and opens onto a private terrace with a
small dipping pool. Electronic amenities in the spacious high-ceilinged rooms include two satellite TVs
with DVD players and computers with Internet access. Guests receive special rates on sightseeing out-
ings aboard the hotel's two cabin cruisers, and Shell
Beach is within walking distance. Because of its wonderful restaurant, the hotel is a member of Gourmet
Hotels of St. Barts, an eight-member group with outstanding chefs who promote classic French cooking.

In St. Jean

★★Eden Rock

St. Jean Beach

☎ 877-563-7105 (US), 590-29-79-99, fax 590-27-88-37, www.edenrockhotel.com

16 suites, cottages, and cabins, plus five "shared-ownership" villas

$$$$

Eden Rock was St. Barts' first hotel (six rooms in the 1950s) and is still one of its finest, thanks to new owners, David and Jane Matthews. It sits on the rock promontory that juts into St. Jean Bay midway down the powdery beach. All the suites are unique, filled with antiques, and feature rock-wall bathrooms. The top accommodations include extras such as plunge pools and private gardens. A new waterside fitness center offers personal health and beauty treatments, and watersports are just steps away on St. Jean beach. The resort is a member of the prestigious Relais & Chateaux (recently merged with Leading Hotels of the World) and Gourmet Hotels of St. Barth. Rates include a  breakfast buffet, airport transfers and use of watersports equipment. The new shared-ownership villas are built next to the original hotel on the site of the old Filao Beach Resort.

★★Tom Beach Hôtel

St. Jean Beach

☎ 590-27-53-13, fax 590-27-53-15, www.tombeach.com

12 rooms

$$$$

AUTHOR'S CHOICE ★ You know when you walk into the quaint little lobby that you are going to have an awesome time. This Créole-style boutique hotel is painted in fire-engine reds, sunburst yellows, and lollipop blues, which makes it stand out on the main road running through St. Jean. Out back, across the bridge that spans the freeform swimming pool, the open-air restaurant (**La Plage**) extends onto the beach (some tables actually sit in the sand), where an energetic young Frenchman tends bar. Each of the spacious rooms has a king-size four-poster bed, a big bathroom with a hair dryer and thick towels, and a private garden patio with a hammock, wet bar, and lounge chairs. Ask for unit eight or nine, which face the beach. Rates include a continental breakfast and airport transfers.

★Hôtel Emeraude Plage

St. Jean Beach

☎ 590-27-64-78; fax 590-27-83-08, www.emeraudeplage.com

24 bungalows, four suites, one villa, two cottages

$$$

You'll be near the airport at this seaside resort, but only small planes go in and out during the day, and all aviation ceases after dark, so you won't be unduly bothered by the noise. The sound of waves breaking on the beach blocks everything else anyway. All units are air conditioned and have ceiling fans, king-size beds and large patios. Each duplex bungalow has a  small kitchenette and the villa and cottages have full kitchens, which makes this a great place if you're planning a long stay or want to eat in to save a little money. On the beach, the Club Eau de Mer serves breakfast and lunch daily.

Hôtel les Islets de la Plage

St. Jean Beach

☎ 590-27-88-57, fax 590-27-88-58

11 one- and two-bedroom bungalows

$$$$

Adorable is the word that best sums up these colorful mini-villas on the beach. All units have lovely teak furniture, even on the covered terrace, which features a well-equipped kitchenette. One-bedroom bungalows have a single spacious bathroom, ceiling fans, and an air-conditioned sleeping area with a queen-size bed. The two-bedroom units have separate bathrooms for each of the air-conditioned bedrooms – one with twin beds, the other with a queen-size bed. Palm trees and flowing bushes extend up the rise from the beach and surround each villa and the swimming pool. Rentals are by the week.

★Le Village St. Jean

Hillside above St. Jean Bay

☎ 590-27-61-39, fax 590-27-77-96, www.villagestjeanhotel.com

Five rooms, 20 cottages, one three-bedroom villa

$$

We think this is among the best bargains on the island. It's not on the beach, but you can walk downhill to the sand in a couple of minutes (going back up takes a tad longer), and the quaint duplex cottages and large infinity pool (no ledge) have great sea views. Inside, everything is sleek with teak and tile throughout. The Charneau family started the village during the 1950s and continue to manage the property, turning first-time visitors into repeaters and friends. Whether you stay in one of the standard hotel rooms outfitted with twin or kingsize beds and a mini-fridge, or one of the large two-bedroom, two-level units with a full kitchen and private patio, you'll enjoy the hospitality as well as the terrific pool, hot tub and gourmet Italian restaurant, **Terrazza**.

Tropical Hotel

Hillside above St. Jean Bay

☎ 590-27-64-87, fax 590-27-81-74, www.tropical-hotel.com

21 rooms

$$

You won't be directly on the beach if you stay here, but you'll be only about 50 yards up a steep road, and nine of the rooms have a view of the sea from their patios. Both the sea-view and garden rooms have kingsize beds draped with totally unnecessary, but romantic, mosquito netting. Every room is air conditioned and furnished with a TV and small refrigerator. A French-style continental breakfast is served pool side every morning, where you'll enjoy a marvelous view of St. Jean Beach. Manager Marithe Weber and her friendly staff go out of their way to make your stay comfortable. The hotel is closed annually from the first of June through mid-July.

On Anse du Grand Cul-de-Sac

★★Le Guanahani

Grand Cul-de-Sac Beach

☎ 590-27-66-60, fax 590-27-70-70; www.leguanahani.com

75 rooms and suites

$$$$

AUTHOR'S CHOICE The Guanahani is unquestionably *magnifique*. In addition to flaunting the highest French star rating, the resort now holds the impressive Five Star Diamond

Award, given to only a few exceptional hotels around the world by the American Academy of Hospitality Sciences for extraordinary quality of service and hospitality. The accolade is not given frivolously and is one of the most coveted international titles. (The Ritz and Le Crillon in Paris, as well as Mar a Lago in Palm Beach, are a few of the 105 hotels that brandish the honor.) The hotel's restaurant and its chef, Philippe Masseglia, are also recognized as Five Star Diamond champions.

So, what does that mean to you, the guest who is spending no less than $700 a night for a prime-time garden-view room? Understated indulgence, *mon cher.*

The oversized compound (75 rooms spread over 16 acres) is huge by St. Barts' standards. But, the resort manages to make every guest feel special in intimate Créole-style cottages, each painted a different tropical color and decorated in white fabrics with soft pastel accents and casual furniture made of fine woods. New flat-screen TVs with DVD players have been placed in every room and the entire resort now has Wi-Fi Internet. The reception area feels more like a friend's seaside cabin than a deluxe resort's lobby, and the wooden decking around the pools lends a rustic quality.

But, make no mistake, this is a high-priced top-notch property and you get plenty of bang for your buck. The beach area is outstanding, spruced up with sculptures, thatched shade umbrellas, plenty of lounge chairs, and a variety of free watersports. When you tire of the beach, you can enjoy complimentary use of the lighted tennis courts and the newly renovated, air-conditioned fitness center. In 2005, the **Guanahani Spa** opened, offering Clarins treatments and Leonor Grey hair care. ☎ 590-52-90-36, www.spaguanahani. com. The concierge takes care of tedious little details, arranging car rentals and sunset cruises. Back in your cottage, room service arrives promptly 24 hours a day.

You'll have little need to leave the property, since **Indigo**, the pool-side café that overlooks the beach, serves a tropical breakfast buffet and marvelous lunches, while the **Bartolomeo Restaurant** serves Provençal-style French dishes for dinner. In the evening, you'll be entertained at **Bar'tô**, a new lounge that offers live music and DJ entertainment. Or, you can simply wander the starlit paths that wind through the landscaped acres of Guanahani's award-winning paradise.

 Guanahani means welcome in the Arawak language.

★★Le Sereno

Grand Cul-de-Sac Beach

☎ 590-29-83-00, fax 590-27-75-47, www.lesereno. com

37 suites and villas

$$$$

This hotel is the work of a talented team lead by world-famous master designer Christian Liaigre. His minimalist style is reflected in the 37 white-walled suites and villas, which are furnished with sleek teak furniture and outfitted with plasma-screen TVs, personal iPods, and Wi-Fi Internet. Beds are made with lush 300-thread-count linens and bathrooms feature thick towels, bathrobes and Ex Voto Paris toiletries. Each unit seems to merge with the magnificently landscaped grounds that front a 600-foot stretch of shade-dappled white-sand beach. A new spa is in the works – it may be accepting clients by the time of your visit – and a fully-equipped health club is open and staffed with trainers. Housekeeping tidies up twice a day and room service delivers around the clock. Should you decide to venture out for a meal, the casual **Restaurant des Pêcheurs** serves a variety of seafood and gourmet dishes throughout the day.

Hôtel les Ondines sur la Plage

Grand Cul-de-Sac Beach

☎ 590-27-69-64, fax 590-52-24-41

Six suites

$$

To stay in the $500 price range (high season), you'll have to settle for a one-bedroom pond-view unit, but that's half the price of a beach-view suite, so it's a real bargain. Suites are open an sunny, with sleek furnishings that lend a modern, minimalist theme. Kitchens are fully equipped, with a built-in dishwasher and French-style clothes washer. Terra cotta tile floors in the living area and bedroom continue right out to furnished patios, which are directly on the sand in beach-side units. Every detail was carefully planned to suit guests who enjoy staying home, and all the facilities of Grand Cul-de-Sac are within walking distance.

Around on the Island

★★Hôtel St. Barth Isle de France

Baie des Flamands

☎ 800-810-4691 (US), 590-27-61-81, fax 590-27-86-83, www.isle-de-france.com

33 rooms and cottages

$$$$

 AUTHOR'S CHOICE The view of stunning Flamands Beach framed by white columns, as you walk into the reception area, will take your breath away. After you recover, you'll realize the rest of the resort lives up to the view.

From the wide beach, an array of hotel rooms and cottages spread up a landscaped hillside.

If you can coax yourself out of your lovely embroidered robe (provided in every room) and out onto the grounds, you'll find a great gourmet French beach-side restaurant (**La Case de l'Île**), two swimming pools, a lighted tennis court, a well-equipped fitness center, the Molten Brown Spa and an upscale boutique filled with top fashion.

Hôtel Manapany

Anse des Cayes

☎ 590-27-66-55, fax 590-27-75-28, www. lemanapany.com

32 cottages

$$$$

Manapany has a legendary reputation as the first luxury hotel on St. Barts. Some say it's showing its age, but style never goes out of style, and Manapany just keeps getting better. Six newer apartments have more room, but every unit is air conditioned and furnished in fine dark woods, and equipped with a large TV and VCR and either a kitchenette or small refrigerator. The main building and **Le Fellini Restaurant** wrap around a lovely pool and deck, and the beach is just steps away. Be aware that some of the cottages are located up the hill from the beach, so don't book one if you don't want to do a little aerobic climbing.

★★Le Toiny

Anse de Toiny

☎ 590-27-88-88, fax 590-27-89-30, www.hotelletoiny.com

15 villas

$$$$

For more than a decade, Le Toiny has been known as one of the priciest resorts in the Caribbean, and repeat guests believe it's well worth every dollar (more than $1,500 per night during season and half that in the summer). We enjoyed a marvelous lunch at the pool-side restaurant, **Le Gaïac**, and snooped around a bit afterwards. We can honestly sum up the resort in one word – WOW.

If you win the lottery, run immediately to the phone and book a room. Any one will do nicely. They all have a private 10 x 20-foot pool, four-poster beds in over-sized bedrooms, rich mahogany furniture handcrafted in Martinique, luxurious bathrooms, and a well-equipped kitchenette. While you're hanging out *chez vous,* you can enjoy two satellite TVs, a VCR, DVD, and a CD player. The only bummer here is that the beach at Anse de Toiny is about a 10-minute walk from the resort, and, once you get there, the water is too rough for swimming.

★La Banane

Lorient Hills

☎ 590-52-03-00, fax 590-27-68-44, www.labanane. com

Nine bungalows

$$$$

The thing that impresses most when you first arrive is all the shade. A palm tree even stands on an island in the middle of the swimming pool. Bungalows are se-cluded in thick tropical vegetation topped by towering trees. The recently refurbished air-conditioned units have Euro-style furniture (including Italian four-poster beds), and DVD players for the TVs. Bathrooms are uniquely designed with open walls onto a private garden or patio and an open-air shower. A two-level swimming pool is tucked into the landscaping; a ten-nis court and restaurant are nearby. You'll have a short walk to Lorient Beach.

★★★★ Christopher

Pointe Milou

☎ 866-287-8017 (US), 590-27-63-63, fax 590-27-92-92

41 rooms

$$$$

There's really no beach at Pointe Milou; the coast is rocky, and the water is too rough for swimming, but don't let that stop you from checking in at this dy-namic hotel. You will get all the water and sun time you need at the huge interconnected double-oval

St. Barts

swimming pool – the largest on the island at 4,500 square feet – an beaches are a 10-minute drive away.

Rooms in this sprawling complex are located in two-story hillside buildings, each with a view of the sea, and each nicely furnished in island-style with TVs, mini-bars, plus patios or balconies.

Hostellerie des Trois Forces

Morne Vivet (the island's highest hill)

☎ 590-27-61-25, fax 590-27-81-38, www.3forces.net

Seven cottages

$

Owner/chef/astrologer Hubert Delamotte and his wife, Ginette, run this 20-year-old New Age resort with love, and they vow that you will leave their hillside

retreat refreshed, transformed, and renewed. Each room is named for and individually designed around a sign of the zodiac, and Hubert will help you choose the unit that will suit you best. All are air conditioned (but you may not need it, since you'll have cooling trade winds), comfortably furnished with four-poster beds, and outfitted with hammocks on a private terrace. If you want to prepare snacks or simple meals in your unit, ask for one with a kitchenette. The rooms are in individual and attached bungalows, and each has a spectacular view of the ocean. Beaches are a five- to 10-minute drive away, but you can relax beside the lovely pool, which is surrounded by a natural-rock deck and padded lounge chairs.

As you would expect, the **restaurant** is gourmet and outstanding. Hubert is an award-winning master chef who puts so much creative spirit into his dishes that he gives *soul food* a whole new meaning. The menu changes and may include Châteaubriand or veal flambée, and vegetarian dishes are always available.

St. Barts

Where to Eat

Allocate a large part of your St. Barts' vacation budget for restaurant meals. The French believe that eating well is the key to living well, and they refuse to live any other way.

Of course, fine dining is rarely inexpensive, and on St. Barts you will be paying for imported foods prepared with great care by talented European-trained chefs. Such meals are improved by the addition of a choice bottle of wine, followed by dessert and a steaming cup of espresso. By the time you purr *L'addition, s'il vous plaît*, your bill will be *très grand*, and worth every euro.

Realizing that your credit card and your waistline may need an occasional change from the typical rich fare, we've also included a few budget-friendly cafés. There are no American-style fast-food joints on St. Barts. Cheap eats are limited to what the French call *les snacks* or *les petits creux* (*creux* means hollow or empty – the state of your stomach, which is remedied by a small meal). These include such things as sandwiches, pizzas, salads and crêpes.

Island Dining

■ You can eat as well on St. Barts as in France. Even little out-of-the-way **cafés** take tremendous pride in serving exquisite cuisine, whether it's French or Créole.

■ Make dinner **reservations**, especially during high season.

■ Call ahead to verify **seasonal** time changes and closings.

■ People dress up a bit for dinner, but shorts and jeans are acceptable at most places during the day. Even the finest restaurants don't require men to wear a jacket or tie, and resort wear is standard at even the finest restaurants.

■ **West Indian** food is typically local vegetables served with fresh seafood. **Créole** adds a spicy mix of African and Caribbean seasonings – and perhaps a slice of grilled goat.

■ Traditional French favorites such as crêpes, quiche, and soupe à l'oignon can be found at some of the small open-air cafés, and *cuisine gastronomique* (a creative mix of French and Créole) is popular in many restaurants.

■ Unless noted otherwise, **restaurant hours** are noon until 3 pm for lunch and 6 until 10:30 pm for dinner. If breakfast is served, the restaurant typically opens at 7 am and serves until 10 am.

■ Nearly all restaurants accept major **credit cards**, with the exception of a few small cafés.

■ Pick up a free copy of *Ti Gourmet* at your hotel or the tourist office. This pocket-sized guide is filled with good restaurant information, including hours of operation and phone numbers, but features only businesses that pay to be included.

Use the scale at right as a guide to what a typical dinner will cost each person, excluding drinks and service charge or tip. Breakfast and lunch prices will be lower.

DINING PRICE CHART	
$	under $20
$$	$21-$30
$$$	$31-$40
$$$$	over $40

No tax is charged on meals. As in France, 15% service charge is included in the price of the meal, but it is customary to leave a small tip. French people usually leave between five and 10% as a *pourboir* ("for drink" in French).

Calling for Reservations

When dialing St. Barts from the US or Canada, dial **011** to get international service, then the area code, **590**, plus the on-island nine-digit number, which means dialing 590 twice (011-590-590-xx-xx-xx).

When calling the islands from Great Britain, dial **00** to get international service first, then follow the above procedure.

On St. Barts or from French St. Martin, you must add a **0** to the nine-digit local number (0590-xx-xx-xx).

Restaurant Directory

GUSTAVIA
Dō Brazil, Shell Beach, ☎ 590-29-06-40 or 590-29-06-66, $$$$
Le Select, Rue du Général de Gaulle, ☎ 590-27-86-87, $
La Sapotillier, Rue de Centenaire, ☎ 590-27-60-28, $$$
Le Repaire, Quai de la République, ☎ 590-27-72-48, $$
La Mandala, Rue Courbet (Rue de la Sous-Préfecture), ☎ 590-27-96-96, $$$
Au Port, Rue du Centenaire, ☎ 590-27-62-36, fax 590-27-97-12, $
Wall House, La Pointe, ☎ 590-27-71-83, $$$
Maya's, Public, West of Gustavia, ☎ 590-27-75-73, $$$$
ST. JEAN
The Hideaway, Chez Andy, ☎ 590-27-63-62, $
La Plage, Tom Beach Hotel, ☎ 590-27-53-13, $$$

St. Barts

Terrazza, Le Village St. Jean Hôtel, ☎ 590-27-70-67, $$$

LORIENT

K'fé Massaï, Oasis Shopping Center, ☎ 590-29-76-78, $$$

POINTE MILOU

Le Ti St-Barth, Pointe Milou Hills, ☎ 590-27-97-71, $$$$

ANSE DES CAYES

Chez Yvon, Main Road, ☎ 590-29-86-81, $$

ANSE DES FLAMANDS

La Langouste, Baie des Anges Hotel, ☎ 590-27-63-61, $$$

In Gustavia

St. Barts' main town has several excellent upscale restaurants and a couple of popular bistros where those in the know hang out and enjoy a good meal.

★★Dõ Brazil

Shell Beach

☎ 590-29-06-40, 590-29-06-66, www.dobrazil.com (in French)

French and Brazilian $$$$

Lunch and dinner daily

Steps lead up from the sand to the open-air dining room that offers a knock-out view of the ocean. Try one of the Brazilian drinks as you watch the sun set, then stay for dinner. Co-owned by Christophe Barjetta (nicknamed Boubou), a Parisian who also owns La Mandala Restaurant, and Yannick Noah, a musician and former tennis star from France, Dõ Brazil adds South American zip and Asian bliss to French cuisine. You'll find lamb with sweet spices and fois gras with mango chutney. Vegetarians will enjoy the Zen menu.

★Le Select

Rue du Général de Gaulle

☎ 590-27-86-87

Burgers and snacks $

Lunch and dinner, Monday-Saturday

Said to be the inspiration for Jimmy Buffet's song, *Cheeseburger in Paradise,* this ultra-casual joint is actually more like a gathering spot for locals and savvy visitors than a restaurant. Still, you can get a beer or cold drink and a cheeseburger (all the sandwiches are very good) and hang out in the shady courtyard while you're waiting for the stores to open for the afternoon. It's also a good place to hear local gossip, find out about new restaurant openings, and perhaps get invited to a party. Most of the patrons will be speaking French, but you won't feel out of place. Activity runs non-stop Monday through Saturday from 10 am until 11 pm.

La Sapotillier

Rue de Centenaire

☎ 590-27-60-28

French/Seafood $$$

Dinner daily

Closed May-October and on Mondays in November and April

Look for this island-style house at the end of the street by Rue du Général de Gaulle. Owner/chef Adam Rajner runs his small restaurant with critical attention to every detail, which wins him many repeat customers. You'll have to call well in advance to get a table under the sapotillier tree (sarsparilla) that dominates the romantic patio.

Outdoor seating is our preference, but you can also dine inside the little cottage, which was moved to the city from the quaint village of Corossol. On our visit, we started by nibbling a superb pâté, moved on to garlicky fish soup, then shared plates of perfectly prepared veal and huge shrimp. Other offerings on the menu included young pigeon flown in from France, frog legs *à la provençale,* and several types of fish served with various sauces. The dishes reminded us of those found in a typical restaurant in Provence.

After lingering over a glass of wine, we had dessert, and highly recommend the apple tart.

Le Repaire

Quai de la République

☎ 590-27-72-48

French and Créole $$

Breakfast, lunch, and dinner daily

You can always get a good meal or refreshing drink at Le Repaire, which means *the den.* The restaurant's complete name is Le Repaire des Rebelles et des Emigrés, but we saw no protesters or exiles in the den on our visits, only some folks playing pool in the back. Everyone else seemed to be there for the well-priced food. We sat facing the marina, people-watching and enjoying mahi mahi and salads. One evening, the menu featured fresh mussels, a personal favorite, and we found them as delicious as those we've had on the French Atlantic coast. The cocktails looked exotic, with lots of fruit and flowers around the glass rim, but we stuck to bottled water, then indulged in ice cream for dessert. If you're in town late at night, the bar and pool tables are open at Le Repaire until midnight.

★★La Mandala

Rue Courbet (Rue de la Sous-Préfecture)

☎ 590-27-96-96, www.lamandala.com

Asian and French $$$

Bar opens daily at 5 pm for tapas

The restaurant serves dinner daily beginning at 7 pm

A mandala is an Oriental design, basically a square inside a circle, that serves as the Buddhist symbol of compassion and universal harmony.

Make reservations for a table on the terrace and arrive before dusk so you can enjoy tapas and drinks while you watch the sun set over the harbor. Stay on for dinner, which may include jumbo shrimp in ginger sauce, curried fish, conch in puff pasty, or selections from the extensive sushi-bar menu. The menu changes to take advantage of the freshest products and showcase the chef's talents.

Au Port

Rue du Centenaire

☎ 590-27-62-36, fax 590-27-97-12

French and Créole $$$$

Dinner only

Closed Sundays and annually in July

On the top floor of a two-story Créole-style building, Au Port claims to be the oldest restaurant on the island. You may think that means out of date and ragged, but Alain Bunel and his congenial staff keep it fresh and welcoming with plants and fresh flowers. The dining area opens onto a lovely balcony overlooking the town, and chef Eric France serves generous portions to keep patrons coming back. The nightly $43 fixed-price Créole meal, which includes wine, is a good choice. Duck is prepared several ways, but we ordered fish and chicken dishes – both were excellent.

★ Wall House

Gustavia, The Point on the Harbor

☎ 590-27-71-83

French and West Indies $$$

Lunch noon-2:30 pm Monday-Saturday, dinner 7-9:30 pm daily

Closed June 1-September 30

While it's possible to run up a large bill at this superb restaurant, there's really no need. Prices are surprisingly moderate, especially for a harbor-side setting overseen by an award-winning chef. If you question your self-restraint, stick to the daily prix fixe offering, which is a bargain. Otherwise, take a leisurely look at the varied menu that includes broiled fish, roasted meats and, our favorite, lobster and grouper lasagna with tomato butter. For a real treat, order the spit roasted chateaubriand for two. Outstanding.

St. Barts

★★Maya's

Public, just outside Gustavia

☎ 590-27-75-73

French and Creole $$$$

Bar opens at 4 pm, dinner 6:30-10:30 pm, Monday-Saturday

Just a short drive from town, and overlooking the sea, Maya's is one of the best places on the island to watch the sunset. Dinner ranges from traditional French items to West Indies favorites spiced with local herbs and peppers. The menu changes regularly, especially during high season, but you'll always find a nice selection of curry and creole dishes. For a more casual meal, at a bit lower cost, try **Maya's To Go** in St. Jean. It's directly across from the airport and has a good selection of take-out food.

For a quick lunch or snack in Gustavia, pick up a crêpe at **La Casa à Crêpes**, Rue de Centeraire, ☎ 590-29-89-70, $

The Top Hotel Restaurants

The following hotel restaurants are not individually reviewed in this guide, but each has a reputation for excellent cuisine prepared by a master chef (usually trained in Europe's finest kitchens) and served in elegant surroundings. Most of the hotels also have more casual cafés that offer equally fine food at more moderate prices.

Bartoloméo, Hôtel Guanahani, Grand Cul-de-Sac, ☎ 590-27-66-60. **L'Indigo**, pool-side at Hôtel Guanahani, is a more casual restaurant serving all day.

La Case de l'Île, Hôtel St. Barth Isle de France, Anse des Flamands, ☎ 590-27-61-81.

Le Gaïac, Hôtel le Toiny, Anse de Toiny, ☎ 590-27-88-88.

Taïno, Hôtel Christopher, Pointe Milou, ℅ 590-27-63-63.

Carl Gustaf Restaurant, Hôtel Carl Gustaf, Gustavia, ☎ 590-27-79-00, fax 590-27-82-37, www.hotelcarlgustaf.com.

The Rock Restaurant, Eden Rock Hotel, St. Jean, ☎ 590-29-79-99, fax 590-27-88-37, www.edenrockhotel.com. (**On the Rock's** serves tapas and splendid cocktails; **The Sand Bar** serves lunch on the beach.)

Restaurant des Pêcheurs, Le Sereno, Grand Cul-de-Sac, ☎ 590-29-83-00, www.lesereno.com.

St. Barts

St. Jean

★La Plage

Tom Beach Hotel

☎ 590-27-53-13

Créole, French, Eclectic $$$

Breakfast, lunch and dinner served daily

Tables spill out of this brilliantly decorated open-air restaurant onto the beach, where you can start your day with fresh-squeezed orange juice and thick French toast. After a morning of watersports, stop back in for a meal-size salad or a hearty sandwich. Créole dishes are the star in the evening, and we suggest you try one of the fresh fish offerings.

Terrazza

Le Village St. Jean Hôtel

☎ 590-27-70-67

Italian $$$

Dinner Thursday-Tuesday

Closed annually in September

We stopped in for pizza one evening and were impressed with the ambitious menu at this indoor/outdoor hotel restaurant. A new chef, Franco Romeao, from Courchevel, France, has taken over the kitchen, which still turns out fragrant homemade breads to accompany every meal. His Italian specialties have been added to the menu, including pan-fried foie gras (good, even if you don't usually care for it pâté-style) and arugula-stuffed veal filet. Expect the menu to change regularly as Romeao adds new dishes, but be assured you can't make a poor selection.

The Hideaway, Chez Andy

St. Jean

☎ 590-27-63-62

Pizza, salads, grilled meat/seafood $

Lunch and dinner Tuesday-Saturday, dinner only on Sunday

Locals told us this casual restaurant was the winner of the Best Pizza Award, so we stopped in at lunchtime to judge for ourselves. We sampled four varieties, and, yes, they are worthy of the prize. Our favorite was the Vivaldi, which came topped with ham, tomato, mozzarella, oregano, red peppers and, the best part, artichoke hearts. A variety of other dishes are on the menu, so spend some time browsing and sipping a cool drink under the ceiling fans before you commit. If you linger long enough, you'll probably spot the friendly English owner, Andy Hall, greeting patrons and accepting praise for both the laid-back atmosphere and delicious food.

Casual, inexpensive meals in St. Jean include sandwiches, fried or grilled fish, and large salads from various cafés in or near the Villa Créole shopping center across the main road from the bay, east of Eden Rock. Our favorites include: Le Pélican, ☎ *590-27-64-64; Le Piment,* ☎ *590-27-53-88;* **Kiki-é-Mo***,* ☎ *590-27-90-65. Also try* **Maya's To Go***,* ☎ *590-27-75-73, a deli with take-out and patio dining at Les Galeries de Commerce shopping center.*

Lorient

★★K'fé Massaï

Oasis Shopping Center

☎ 590-29-76-78

French Contemporary $$$

Dinner daily

No credit cards

AUTHOR'S CHOICE ★ Put this African-themed café and bar on your list. It's currently one of the island's hot spots for trendy locals. Co-owners Pascal Vallon (everyone calls him Pinpin) and Hervé Chovet put special emphasis on high quality at an affordable price, and we give them four stars for succeeding. K'fé Massaï serves matchless nouveau-French cuisine with Asian and Caribbean accents. The décor features dark wood and captivating African sculpture, designed to draw you in and entice you to stay. Comfortable lounge areas open onto a lush garden, and custom-designed tables and chairs add to the ethnic ambience of the dining room. Still, it's the intriguing food that will keep you coming back for more. We started with marinated peppers and zucchini stuffed with fresh goat cheese and a vegetable tartare with smoked salmon. Fresh French bread was already on the table. All the main courses sounded delicious, but we finally settled on pan-seared tuna and

St. Barts

a Thai-style chicken brochette. Both were excellent, and people dining nearby gave two thumbs up for their beef filet dinners. Dessert would have been a difficult decision, except that we're chocolate fiends and went straight for the banana-spiked chocolate mousse. Excellent choice.

Author's Tip: *For a quick lunch or light dinner, try **Le Bouchon**, in the same shopping center as K'fe Massai. Burgers, fries and salads are the best bet, but they also offer pizza. Open daily 11 am-10 pm,* ☎ *590-27-79-39.*

Pointe Milou

Le Ti St-Barth

Pointe Milou Hills

☎ 590-27-97-71

Steaks, Créole, Eclectic $$$$

Dinner daily 7:30-11 pm; bar open at 7 pm

Billing itself as a Caribbean tavern, this wild and crazy restaurant is a favorite with the young and untamed. Full-moon parties and outlandish theme nights draw a huge crowd, so you'll need a reservation most evenings, especially if you want to book a prime table in the torch-lit covered courtyard. A surly-faced pirate is the mascot (probably famous Barth-bad-boy, Montbars the Exterminator) and the décor could be straight off a buccaneer-movie set.

On the night we stopped in (after navigating up the steep cliffhanger road to the top of the hill overlooking Pointe Milou), prime rib for two was the big seller, but the ambitious menu also offered seafood and chicken, as well as snail cassoulet and crayfish fricassée. A great mix of lively music was playing, and vanilla rum flowed freely, so we weren't surprised when people began dancing on the tables.

Thierry DeBadereau and Carole Gruson, who own the colorful Tom Beach Hotel and its eclectic La Plage restaurant, are the masterminds behind Ti's overwhelming success.

St. Barts

Anse des Cayes

Chez Yvon

Main Road

☎ 590-29-86-81

Creole $$

Lunch and dinner daily

Check out the daily special (*plat du jour*) that's written on a board beside the menu posted outside the front door. You'll likely find a French favorite, such as boeuf bourguignonne, prepared with a Caribbean twist. The main menu features salads, quiche, and crêpes.

 Most restaurants close annually for several weeks and curtail serving hours during the low season. Always call ahead to verify hours of operation.

Anse des Flamands

La Langouste

Baie des Anges Hotel

☎ 590-27-63-61

Seafood, Créole, and French $$$

Lunch and dinner served daily during high season

Langouste is the French word for spiny lobster, so we recommend you give special attention to the seafood selections. The lobster salad made with fresh grapefruit is a mouth-tingling treat on a warm day, and the stuffed crab has a lot of zing. Interior decorations reflect a nautical theme, and you'll have a view from your table of lavish yachts moored in the cove.

Nightlife

Nightlife on St. Barts is considerably quieter than on St. Martin. There are no casinos or movie theaters, and only a few hotels offer evening entertainment; even that is more along the lines of piano music, rather than disco or a full-production floor show. If you need a lot of all-night action, this may not be the island for you.

However, there are a few lively hot spots, especially during the winter tourist season, and many restaurant bars stay open after dinner hours. You can find out about theme nights and visiting entertainers performing at trendy clubs by browsing through the free publications, **Le Journal de St. Barth, Saint-Barth Weekly** and **Ti-Gourmet**.

Locals enjoy drinks and conversation Monday through Saturday at **Le Select** on the corner of Rue de la France and Rue du Général de Gaulle, a block inland from the Gustavia harbor, ☎ 590-27-86-87. Join in by ordering a drink and settling in at one of the tables scattered under the trees in the graveled courtyard. This isn't a late-night spot, since the bar closes at 11 pm, but prices are low, and it's a great place to meet people.

Diagonally across the road, **Bar de l'Oubli** is a bit more chic, but still closes at 11 pm. It's right across from the harbor on Rue de la République, ☎ 590-27-70-06.

Bête à Z'ailes, also on the Gustavia harbor, is known as a sushi/ martini/wine bar that hosts great live music shows. You can check out their schedule of entertainment in the free weeklies or online at www.bazbar.com. During high season, you may find as many celebrities seated in the audience as on stage. ☎ 590-29-74-09.

In the village of Lurin, live music and dancing begins around 10 am at **Feeling**, ☎ 590-27-88-67. Call ahead to find out who's playing. It's open until 2 or 3 am.

Nikki Beach

St. Jean has a couple of popular night spots with scheduled entertainment, including **La Plage** at Tom Beach Hotel, ☎ 590-27-53-13, **Zanzibarth**, ☎ 590-27-53-00, and **Nikki Beach**, ☎ 590-27-64-64.

Bar'tô at the Guanahani Hotel in Grand Cul-de-Sac features guest entertainers and lounge music. ☎ 590-27-70-70.

Island Facts & Numbers

AIRPORT CODE: SBH

AREA CODE: 590 (see *Telephone* below).

ATMS & BANKS:

Banque National de Paris, Boulevard du Bord de Mer, Gustavia.

Banque Française Commerciale, Rue du Général de Gaulle, Gustavia, ☎ 590-27-62-62.

Banque Française Commerciale, Galeries du Commerce, St. Jean, ☎ 590-27-65-88.

BUS: Mini-bus service is provided by **Le Shuttle** throughout the island for €10 roundtrip. It runs from 9-1 am daily. ☎ 590-29-44-19.

CAPITAL: Gustavia.

CREDIT CARDS: Widely accepted by most businesses, but ask before you shop if the credit card symbol is not displayed in the window.

DEPARTURE TAX: $15 when going to another French island; $10 when going elsewhere. Cash only, in dollars or Euros.

ELECTRICITY: 220 V-60 Hz (products made for use in North America require a current transformer and plug converter; those made for use in Europe may run hot).

EMERGENCY NUMBERS: **Fire, Police, Medical Emergency**, ☎ 18 (do not dial 0 first).

For non-emergencies: **Fire**, ☎ 590-27-66-13; **Police**, ☎ 590-27-11-70; **Sea Rescue**, ☎ 596-70-92-92; **Doctor** on call, ☎ 590-27-76-03; **Hospital**, ☎ 590-27-60-35.

GAS STATIONS: St. Jean, Main Road near Galleries du Commerce, Monday-Saturday, 7:30 am-5 pm, ☎ 590-27-50-50; Lorient, Main road, Monday-Friday, 7:30 am-5 pm, and Saturday, 7:30 am-5:30 pm, ☎ 590-27-62-30.

HIGHEST POINT: Morne du Vitet at 938 feet.

LAND AREA: Eight square miles.

LANGUAGE: French; many residents also speak English.

MONEY: Euro, but the US dollar is accepted in most places.

NEWSPAPER: *Le Journal de Saint Barth*, in French, and *Saint-Barth Weekly*, in English, are free weekly publications. Both list current events and local happenings. *Le News* and *L'Essentiel* are French dailies, with *Le News* featuring condensed news from France, while *L'Essentiel* offers expanded international stories. Look for a complimentary copy of *Ti-Gourmet Saint-Barth* to find restaurant reviews and information about evening entertainment, cultural events and happy hours.

PHARMACIES: **Pharmacie St. Barth**, ☎ 590-27-61-82 (in Gustavia, across from the ferry dock); **Pharmacie de L'Aéroport**, ☎ 590-27-66-61 (across from the airport); **Island Pharmacie**, ☎ 590-29-02-12 (in St. Jean).

POLITICAL STATUS: The island is politically tied to the island of Guadeloupe, which is an Overseas Region of France.

POPULATION: Approximately 7,000.

POST OFFICES: **Gustavia**, corner of Rue Fahlberg and Rue Jeanne d'Arc, ☎ 590-27-62-62; **St. Jeanne**, Galeries du Commerce; **Lorient**, Main Road.

RADIO STATIONS: **Radio Saint-Barth**, 103.7 FM, ☎ 590-27-74-74; **Radio Transat**, 100.3 FM, ☎ 590-27-60-62.

RELIGIOUS SERVICES: **Catholic**, Rue Courbet, Gustavia and Main Road, Lorient (services at each church on alternating weeks, call for the schedule), 5:30 pm Saturday and 8 am Sunday, ☎ 590-27-61-08. **Anglican**, Gustavia, 9 am Sunday, ☎ 590-27-89-44. Gustavia (call for the schedule), ☎ 590-27-61-60.

TAXIS: Taxis are plentiful at the airport and ferry docks. Drivers are licensed by the government and carry a published rate sheet, which lists authorized fares between many common destinations, such as from the airport to major hotels. Ask to see it. Daytime rates apply from 7 am to 9 pm. An additional 25% is

St. Barts

added to the base fare from 9 until midnight; 50% is added to the base fare from midnight to 7 am. If your destination isn't listed, negotiate a price before you get into the cab, and confirm whether the rate is quoted per trip or per passenger.

Unless the driver overcharges, is rude, or takes you out of your way, plan to add at least a 10% tip to the fare. Tip a little extra if the driver gives information about the island as you travel or helps you with your luggage (50¢ to $1 per bag is standard, depending on the size and weight of each piece). US dollars and euros are accepted, but don't expect the driver to have change for large-denomination bills. **Taxi Dispatch**, ☎ 590-27-75-81 (airport) or 590-27-66-31 (Gustavia).

TELEPHONE:

 You must add a 0 to the beginning of each number when you dial locally. Example: 0590-xx-xx-xx.

■ When dialing St. Barts from the US or Canada, dial 011 to get international service, then the area code, 590, plus the on-island nine-digit number, which means dialing 590 twice (011-590-590-xx-xx-xx). When calling St. Barts from Great Britain, dial 00 to get international service, then follow the above procedure.

■ Within the overseas French system, you must add a 0 to the nine-digit local number; so, to call French St. Martin, dial 0590-xx-xx-xx.

■ To call out from St. Barts to an island in the Netherlands Antilles, dial 00 + area code + local number. So, to call Dutch St. Martin, dial 00 + 599 + xxx-xxxx.

■ To call an island or country not in the overseas French system or in the Netherlands Antilles, dial 00, then the country code + area code + the local number. As an example, to call the US or Canada, dial 00 + 1 + area code + local number. To call anywhere in Great Britain, dial 00 + 44 + the number.

■ You will find all country codes listed along with long-distance rates in the TELEDOM phone directory that's available at all hotels.

■ **Cell phones** are a good idea, especially if you plan to make a lot of calls back home or to neighboring islands. **East Caribbean Cellular** covers St. Barts and St. Martin, ☎ 599-542-2100, www. eastcaribbeancellular.com.

TELEPHONE CARDS: Most public phones are not coin-operated, but require a telephone card, which can be purchased at a post office, gas station, or convenience store. Some phones accept major credit cards.

TELEPHONE OPERATOR: ☎ 12.

TEMPERATURE RANGE: Year-round average low is 72°F; year-round average high is 86°F.

TIME: St. Barts is on Atlantic Standard Time and doesn't observe Daylight Savings Time. During the summer months, island time is the same as Eastern Daylight Time; in the winter, island time is one hour ahead. St. Barts' time is five hours behind England and six hours behind France and the rest of Western Europe during the summer; it's four hours behind England and five hour behind western Europe in the winter.

TIPPING IN RESTAURANTS: On St. Barts, as in France, a service charge is added to the price of each item on the menu. Most people leave an additional five-10% on the table for the server, since the service charge is divided among all employees. If service is poor, tell the manager or owner of the restaurant. Failing to leave a tip does nothing to correct the problem.

TOURIST OFFICE: Office Municipal du Tourisme de Saint-Barthèlemy, located at Rue de la République, harbor side, open Monday-Friday, 8:30 am-12:30 pm and 2:30-5:30 pm, Saturday, 9:30-11:30 am, ☎ 590-27-87-27, fax 590-27-74-47, www.saint-barths.com.

In the US

French Government Tourist Office, 444 Madison Avenue, 16th Floor, New York, NY 10022, ☎ 212-838-

7800, fax 212-838-7855, www.francetourism.com, info@francetourism.com.

In Canada

French Government Tourist Office, 1981 Avenue McGill College, Ste 490, Montreal, Québec QU H3A 2W0, ☎ 514-288-4264, fax 514-844-8901, valerie. ammann@mdlfr.com.

WATER: It's safe to drink, but most people prefer bottled water, which is readily available. Drinking water is rainfall collected in cisterns or desalinated sea water.

WEBSITES: www.St-Barths.com is the official Tourist Office site. You might also want to check www. frenchcaribbean.com, www.sbhonline.com and www. gotostbarths.com..

WiFi: WiFi hotspots are becoming common throughout Gustavia. Many restaurants and resorts offer laptop access, including Do Brasil, Le Select, Le Square, Kiki-e-Mo, L'Oasis Shopping Center, Villa Créole, Le Flamboyant Tennis Club, Maya's To Go and Brasserie La Repaire. You can buy HotSpot access through St Barth Telecom.

Index